Out of the Courtroom Into the Father's House

Allyn Benedict

ISBN: 978-0-9565717-3-1

Out of the Courtroom
into The Father's House

Published and distributed by The Maranatha Community Trust
102 Irlam Road, Flixton, Manchester M41 6JT
Tel: 0161 748 4858 Fax: 0161 747 7379
email: info@maranathacommunity.org.uk
www.maranathacommunity.org.uk

For information address:
The Maranatha Community UK Office
102 Irlam Road, Flixton, Manchester M41 6JT
Tel: 0161 748 4858 Fax: 0161 747 7379
email: info@maranathacommunity.org.uk
www.maranathacommunity.org.uk

ISBN: 978-0-9565717-3-1

Printed in the United Kingdom 2011

Commendations

Human life is torn apart by conflicts which are never resolved and every page of our history is marked by Man's inhumanity to man. In his deeply insightful and prophetic book Allyn Benedict shows that Idolatry – a counterfeit judge – is at the centre of the human heart. We are living in bondage to a legal system which is deeply flawed, and we discover that such bondage expresses itself in self-righteousness. Consider the broken history of Ireland and the terrible consequences of political judgements which are not rooted in Gospel truth.

That truth is revealed with clarity in the powerful prophetic vision of the courtroom granted to Allyn Benedict in 2001. "This courtroom was, in truth, the world itself – our universal, fallen human condition." Jesus enters the courtroom surrounded by light. To step into this light is to be set free from the legal systems of this world. Legalism with all of its ramifications will undermine the powerful message of the Christian Gospel and lead us into the judgement of this world where Jesus the Christ is not enthroned as the King of Kings and Lord of Lords.

Father William Keogh, English Martyrs' Roman Catholic Church. Kent, England

Contents

INTRODUCTION

A word for the Church

Most Christians who have been involved in any significant way in the life of a local congregation are acquainted with these persistent and destructive patterns of behaviour: the person who finds fault with everything and everyone; the one who sows discord and gossip; the one who is easily offended; the person who becomes the centre of a "faction" which draws its destructive, divisive energy and focus from some perceived offence to justice, rightness or fairness; the person (often a leader) who cannot abide any criticism, no matter how constructive; the one who must "get his own way" regardless of the cost or means, be it manipulation or intimidation. The list could go on. Right alongside many wonderful manifestations of God's transforming grace, the church, in all its expressions, continues to live with the consequences of human bitterness, defensiveness, unforgiveness, arrogance, insecurity, contempt, self-centredness and self-hatred. Not only are these patterns persistent, but many times they occur in such subtle ways - often under the cover of Christian vocabulary - that we are blinded by the destruction of relationships and the undermining of effective ministries: we didn't see it coming; we have very little awareness of where the destructive power is rooted.

The foundational teaching of this book concerns the origin of the destructive patterns described above. The power behind these patterns, observable in both the world and in the Church, is nothing less than the life-destroying power of idolatry. There is an idol worshipped at the centre of the human heart: a judge; a deceived, rebellious, counterfeit judge. "In Adam", humanity sits in judgement - each one over his or her own life - idolatrous judges in a fallen world that is, in truth, a courtroom.

For a Christian, it cannot be surprising that this idolatry reigns in the world. But I believe that we cannot become the Church which glorifies the Father *in and through the concrete content of the actual life we live together for him,* unless we come to terms with the fact that the destructive ways and means of judgement are easily observable in the life and witness of the Church and its members. We claim that we are "sons", yet too often we do not live in freedom as sons and daughters of our Father. Rather, we find ourselves living in bondage to a legal system, living out courtroom roles as judges, prosecutors, defendants and witnesses. We are constantly gathering evidence in our struggle to secure for ourselves what God seeks to restore to us by adoption and grace: personal identity, provision and purpose.

The destructive power of human judgement is rooted in the human heart - in every heart where Jesus Christ is *not* enthroned as the only judge. There, in each of our hearts, Jesus is coming to set us free. If we seek to be servants of the living God - if we desire to know a greater hunger to follow Jesus Christ as Lord and to live his life - we must come to terms with this truth: *unless Jesus is our only judge, he is not our only Lord.*

Judgement: the enemy of spiritual life

The scriptural revelation concerning the human tendency to enter into the kind of judgement which stands in opposition to God's word and will can be summed up in this one clear statement: "Do not judge, or you too will be judged" [Matthew 7:1].

Two kinds of judgement

It is vitally important that we understand the kind of judging to which Jesus refers in this passage, and which Paul invokes when

2

he writes, "Therefore let us stop passing judgement on one another [Romans 14:13]". Does scripture prohibit us from ever making any kind of judgements about people? Clearly this is not the case. Scripture everywhere acknowledges that we must make judgements. Jesus, who says "do not judge", tells us to make "a right judgement", and commands us to "stop judging by mere appearances" [John 7:24]. Paul says emphatically, "… let us stop passing judgement on one another" [Romans 14:13], but to the Corinthians he says, "Are you not to judge those inside [the church]…Expel the wicked man from among you" [1 Corinthians 5:12b, 13b]. Paul tells the church in Corinth that he does not judge himself [1 Corinthians 4:3b], yet he warns them later *in the same letter* that if they would only judge themselves they would not come under judgement [11:31]! Is Paul inconsistent? Is Jesus? To quote Paul: "By no means"! The scriptural guidance and exhortation which calls for the exercise of *appropriate* human judgement refers to a kind of *permitted* judgement which is significantly different from the kind which is *prohibited*.

As human beings, especially as Christians, we must necessarily make the "judgements" permitted in scripture about a great many things including the behaviour of others. Paul refers in the example above to the kind of judgements which must be made in the Body of Christ. Surely this is the case in our personal lives as well. For example, we cannot care for our children unless we protect them, as much as we are able, from things that are harmful. It is certainly possible for me to make judgements that lead me to conclude that a particular person cannot be trusted with my 12 year old daughter *without breaking Jesus' commandment, "do not judge"*. This would be a "judging" which is both permitted and necessary. But it is also possible that I could protect my daughter *and* enter into destructive, prohibited judgement of the person from whom I am protecting her. If I break Jesus' commandment by entering into this destructive kind of judging, I may protect her from one kind of harm, but I expose her to another.

And what if someone actually hurts my daughter, perhaps very seriously, as with a sexual assault? I may judge that action as evil and see the powerfully destructive potential of it for her present and her future, for the one who hurt her and even for others not directly involved. I may believe that the guilty person should be held accountable in a variety of ways, including legally. It may be that I see some roots of this destructive act in the sinful systems of this world. I may even come to understand that I have not been as aware as I should be of the dangers that she confronts in her world and/or that I am at fault in not paying attention to clear warnings that this person was not safe. Again: I can I enter into the many "judgements" involved in all these things without breaking Jesus' commandment not to judge. But it is also possible that I might take an entirely different path. In the face of the very same circumstances, I may enter into bitter and destructive judgement of the person who hurt my daughter, of others I blame, of myself, of the systems of this world and of God! Having entered this bitter path, I might even end up blaming and judging my daughter.

In the circumstance just described, as in so many arenas of real life, it was necessary to make judgements. But the kind of judgements entered into would make all the difference. Though they would be taken in response to the same circumstance, the two paths of judgement just described would go two very different places. On the first path - permitted and necessary judgement - we can walk together with Jesus in love and truth. But the path of prohibited, destructive judgement is the way of isolation and estrangement - we walk that way alone and apart from both truth and love. These paths are as different as day and night. One leads to blessing and life; the other to cursing and death.

"Matthew 7 Judgement"

The judging which Jesus speaks of in Matthew 7 can be described as: *a "courtroom" orientation and activity presided over by one who assumes the idolatrous position of judge over his or her own life.* This is in sharp contrast to the judgement which is permitted, which can be described as *a biblically based discernment of good and evil concerning human behaviour - a "judging" made in God's will and exercised to fulfil his purposes.*

For most of us, even those who have walked with Jesus for many years, judgement rooted in this *courtroom orientation* is a significant part of our lives. It remains there as a fundamental part of our disposition towards ourselves and others, but we fail to see it for what it is. "Matthew 7 judgement" is our deadly, but unexamined enemy. It robs us of much of our freedom in Jesus Christ, and severely inhibits our formation into his likeness.

The difficulties we face in coming to recognize and accept this truth are many. A good illustration of this came when I first began to preach on the subject. There was a young woman in the congregation (a faithful wife and mother who had come to the Lord in her early twenties) who had become aware of some deeply rooted brokenness and oppression in her life. She had suffered and struggled for years but was being touched by God's truth and mercy. Healing, forgiveness and transformation were underway and she had a growing witness of God's power coming to set her free. She remembers clearly (and with a smile) her reaction to my first sermon about the ways of judgement in the human heart: "When Pastor preached about judgement, I thought, 'Whew! Well, that's a relief! I've got everything else wrong with me, but at least I don't have a problem with that!'"

She didn't know what she didn't know. But she was open to Jesus' saving work in her. She was used to meeting with him in his word and in prayer concerning the condition of her heart. And, sure enough, Jesus began to show her the judgement that lived in oppressive power there. As is often the case, once the process of recognition got started she began to see it everywhere! In a very short time she came to understand that judgement was at the root of all that had held her in bondage since her childhood. The beginning of the end of its power in her life came when it was exposed to the light. The foundation of its strength lay in being hidden.

Judgement: the hidden enemy

Our most dangerous enemy is often the one we do not see. This is the case with prohibited judgement. It can come so deceptively that we are literally blind to both the judgement itself and its fruit. Often it comes in an attractively wrapped "package" which our flesh finds impossible not to open. It feels so incredibly satisfying! When we enter into destructive judgement, it can not only feel *good*, but *right*! We would not question it, but more than that, we would vigorously defend our exercise of it both as our *right* and even as our *duty*!

Although "Matthew 7" judgement can yield obvious and devastating results, it often comes in forms that simply look like common, ordinary, everyday ways of human life that we accept without question. We dismiss what we see as no judgement at all, or as trivial, at least by comparison with more lurid examples of judgement we see or read about. After hearing some common examples of judgement as it crops up (even in our own life) one can begin to think, "Why that's not an example of idolatry; that's just an example of being human!" Exactly. That is the theme of this book: every human person lives as an idol in "the courtroom" until the mercy of God enters into the world - that is, until the coming of Jesus

Christ *and his enthronement on the judgement seat of the human heart.*

It is important to recognize that when we experience mild symptoms of the fallen human condition it can be like experiencing a relatively minor physical symptom of a deadly disease. The symptom may get our attention but it does not exist in isolation. It is part of a network of active corruption that will take our life if ignored.

When we enter into destructive judgement, that judging is a symptom. Throughout the course of this book, we will look closely at the symptoms, exploring the effects of judgement. We will see it in its most blatant forms, and learn to see its face in the ordinary things of daily life. However, though our symptomatic suffering and our symptomatic sinning matters to Jesus, he has come as our Saviour to address the *disease at the root of both.* When we enter into destructive judgement, the symptoms mask the true and desperate condition we are in: *the only Righteous Judge is not on the judgement seat of our lives.*

Judgement: The way of freedom

Scripture reveals that it is not the will of God that we would remain in bondage to anything other than his righteousness and his mercy and that our death does not please him. It is his desire that we "turn from our wickedness and live". That turning must involve, at the core, our getting down off the seat of judgement so that Jesus can take his place, not only as our Saviour and Lord, but as our *only* Judge. Again, this is critical: unless and until he is our only judge he cannot be our only Saviour or our only Lord and an idol remains at the centre of our life, personally and corporately. We are that idol!

The good news is this: though he must be on the judgement seat of each of our lives, Jesus has not come to take that seat in order to judge us, but in order to save us [John 12:47]. His primary work in us brings us out of idolatry - out of captivity to the judgement which enslaves the kingdom of this world - into the Kingdom of God, where we live with an unpayable debt to the Father's mercy, in the marvellous light and freedom known only to those who are receiving the power to become the children of God [John 1:12].

BOOK ONE:
THE COURTROOM

Part One

In The Courtroom:
The Way It Looks From Here

✝

Chapter 1

THE COURTROOM:
A Revelation

In the autumn of 2001 I received a revelation from God concerning judgement in the human heart. This did not come to me as a direct response to some question I had or some understanding I was seeking. Nor was it an insight that served a teaching I was preparing. I was simply standing on the chancel steps of the church where I was serving, looking out on the stone, wood, tile and stained glass of the nave. I remember being very aware of God's presence; I felt full and expectant at the same time. It was a Saturday morning and I was opening myself to God's word in preparation for preaching the next day. But what came had nothing directly to do with the scriptures for that day.

I want to emphasize that the vision and understanding that came to me was nothing new: the revelations that the Father gives to his children are not some "new" word in the sense of "adding" something to scripture. They are a new *path*, perhaps, into his perfect and timeless word. He reveals connections and understandings which may be "new" to a given generation. He unfolds implications in a fresh new way. But all he is doing is continuing to water, in us, the wonderful and imperishable seed of his living word.

All the world a courtroom!

As I stood there that morning, the nave of Christ Church ceased to be a nave: it became a courtroom. I saw galleries and an imposing raised dais for the judge with a huge chair and a desk complete with gavel. A railed witness platform and chair was nearby. There was a large panelled jury box and many tables with chairs for all the large cast of characters common to courtrooms; for prosecutors and plaintiffs, defendants with their lawyers, and for all the usual court functionaries: stenographers, bailiffs, clerks, reporters and so on. All was on a grand scale with the Norman columns and arching wood beams adding solidity to the picture in my mind.

As I was being given this vision, I was also being filled with an awareness of its significance. This "courtroom" was, in truth, the world itself. The walls and vaulted ceiling of the church became the physical confines of this world and therefore the context of every earthly human life. I also knew that this was a vision of the *spiritual* confines and context of human life; not just one of the possibilities, but rather the universal "fallen" human condition.

Although there were many dynamics to this scene, many roles being played out and a great deal of activity, it was clearly a vision of bondage: the courtroom was a prison. There was no alternative place to go, regardless of any human efforts that could be made. I knew that we are born into this courtroom, we live in it and we die in it. This is our world. This is our life, and yet …

Light in the courtroom

And yet, as I watched, Jesus entered the courtroom. I saw that where he stood there was a cone of light. It seemed to be coming from him; it surrounded him and extended up into the heavens. I had not seen the darkness of the courtroom until he entered as light. I understood that to step into his light was to be set free. I had an awareness that this meant a new identity. One would no longer be captive to the legal system that is this world - but the courtroom remained there all around, still a seductive option, even for those who came to Jesus.

Though we could come into the cone of light with Jesus, I knew that there was no "way out" of the courtroom in the physical sense. Not for Jesus any more than for us. The exit Jesus would have to take from the courtroom would have to be the same as our exit: physical death.

But he was not a prisoner here. He had entered in perfect freedom and great power. Jesus had the power to be in the courtroom but remain who he was. He was free to be the Father's child. This same freedom was what he offered every captive there. All people could draw near and come into his light. There with him, though still *in* the courtroom, one would no longer have to be *of* it; no more adopting courtroom roles; no more living with a legal orientation.

I saw the whole world as one big courtroom, but I understood and saw that each person presides as judge over his or her own personal courtroom as a counterfeit judge.

A gift of sight

This revelation came, I believe, as a gift of sight: the courtroom was a way of seeing a basic orientation of the human heart. It was a way of seeing clearly all the ways of judgement from the most common and apparently trivial to the most dramatic and obviously devastating extremes. But whether it appeared in bland or lurid manifestations, or somewhere in between, judgement in all its guises could easily be seen as fruit of a common tree.

With the vision of the courtroom came an invitation: look at what goes on in a courtroom; see who is there and what they do. I began to examine my own heart with Jesus in the light of the new understanding that came as I looked. I began to preach about judgement. And as I shared this with brothers and sisters in Christ, we began to look together. This was literally awesome! The Lord took the reality of judgement as an abstract concept and gave it concrete form for us - something very familiar from everyday life. And yet the key was not so much the courtroom as it was the ways and means of the legal system itself: its procedures, objectives and, especially, the roles played out there.

Many times awareness and insight come with great struggle and significant cost - this was *not* such a time! The struggles have certainly come, and the cost has been counted as we have sought to receive the power to be set free and to walk in the truth. But in the beginning, fresh new connections and understanding continued to be heaped on us. It was an amazing experience. It was exhilarating!

It was also devastating! Insights into the ways of judgement came as hammer blows. There was no way to stand apart in a safe place. The *universal* implications were obvious and the *personal* application meant the end of "business as usual" for anyone who took the time to be examined in this light, with this new way of seeing.

However, from the first days until the present, the experience of being with Jesus *together*, looking at the paths of judgement in the human heart (in our hearts), sharing experiences and insights, sharing in the scriptures that have always been there revealing the truth about the roots, and ways, and bondage of judgement, but which we now see and hear more clearly - all of this was what I can only describe as koinonia: fellowship in the Spirit as we received a great gift together. There is joy in the midst of the suffering required of those who would, "by the Spirit of God, put to death the works of the flesh." It was and is a blessed way to walk together, because the road of freedom is the road of joy. We've experienced again the truth that Jesus is our joy, because he not only opened the way out of the courtroom and into the Father's house, but is himself that Way and our companion on the road.

Chapter 2

THE COURTROOM:
Life as we know it

"Fred and Jane"

Prologue
[The phone rings at Fred's house: Jane, his sister, is calling]

Fred: Hello.
Jane: Fred! It's Jane.
Fred: Jane! What's up?
Jane: I was going to leave a message; I'm surprised you're home.
Fred: How come?
Jane: I thought you were going to visit Mum this afternoon.
Fred: *(shocked)* Oh no!
Jane: You said you were going to call her.
Fred: I did call her! I forgot to go!!
Jane: You're kidding!
Fred: No! I completely forgot!
(silence)
Jane: You promised her.
Fred: I know. I can't believe I did this.

Jane: Well I can believe it! You did the same thing last year…and on her birthday, for heaven's sake!

(silence)

Well… look, it's not the end of the world. She'll get over it.

(silence)

Really.

But you'd better make it up to her.

(silence)

Listen, I've got to go. Just wanted you to know that Dave and I want you guys over for dinner on Friday. OK?

Fred: Yeah. Fine.

Jane: Great, we'll talk.

Fred: Ok.

Jane: Bye.

Fred: Bye.

Scene 1

[Things continue at Fred's house]

Fred: I can't believe I did it again! How can I be so stupid? How could I be so thoughtless? I'm a miserable excuse for a son. Why do I do this? What is wrong with me? I know how lonely mum is…she's alone most of the time. I know how much a visit means to her. She was waiting for me. She's probably still waiting. Will she ever forgive me? I can't imagine what she thinks of me. She'll probably give me the silent treatment now. Jane's right: it's not the first time. I actually forgot her birthday last year. When I think of all she's gone through: She practically died when I was born! Some gratitude this is! I hate myself!

Scene 2

[Meanwhile at Jane's house]

Jane: He *better* make it up to her. Oh Lord, it's going to take mum a long time to get over this one. Of course, with mum, Fred can do no wrong. She'll probably find a way to make it my fault. *He* forgets… but somehow it's *my* fault. She always turns it around. And I end up apologizing because he's a crummy son. He's always doing this to me. I don't think he even cares about her. He certainly doesn't care about me. Fred cares about Fred. The last time I gave him a birthday present he didn't even thank me. He doesn't want to know about all the stuff I do for mum. How does he think she does her laundry? Who does he think changes her bed? Who buys her medicine? Who buys her food? Is he ever there when she's crying about how lonely she is? And then he forgets her birthday! I carry the whole responsibility of keeping this family together. And nobody cooperates; not Fred; not that woman he married; not mum. And that husband of mine? Forget about it!

Scene 3

[At Fred's house; his wife, Fran, enters]

Fred: I can't believe it!
Fran: What are you so upset about?
Fred: How could I treat my own mother this way when she worked that rotten job for 12 years just to save money to put me through college?
Fran: Yeah and she never lets you forget it.
Fred: I forgot to visit her today. Just like last year, on her birthday!
Fran: So?
Fred: So Jane called and reminded me.

Fran: Oh, so "Miss Perfect" called!

Fred: It's not her fault. She was just trying to leave a message to invite us to dinner. She was surprised I was home.

Fran: Yeah? When was the last time she remembered your birthday?

Fred: Well she's busy with the kids.

Fran: Busy?! They're in school all day. What does she have to do? Watch soap operas? This is your only day off! You've got a full time job. The pressure never lets up! No wonder you forget things once in a while.

Fred: Yeah. You know what? You're right! The last time she remembered my birthday, it had to be 5 years ago. She gave me a £3.00 "soap-on-a-rope." And I gave her a £20 gift certificate. And she has to remind me that I forgot mum's birthday… *last year*! She always does stuff like that. She finds every little thing I do wrong and makes sure I know about it.

Fran: You said it!

Fred: What does she mean "I forget mum all the time"? I'm always doing stuff for mum.

Fran: Right!

Fred: What about the fact that I fixed her refrigerator last month?

Fran: Who does Jane think took care of that mess with your mum's bank account? What has she ever done?

Fred: Yeah; except point out my faults. You know what she admitted to me? *[conspiratorially:]* Last month she completely forgot to pick up her kids from school.

Fran: No!

Fred: Yes! They sat out on the curb for 2 hours. The custodian found them and they had to call around looking for her.

Fran: Unbelievable!

Scene 4:
[At Jane's house]

Jane: I don't believe this! I have to go over there and take care of mum's laundry tomorrow. I'm going to have to listen to her sob story about how her son stood her up.

[Jane's husband, Dave, enters]

Dave: What's your mother moaning about now?

Jane: Fred forgot to go visit mum today. Again.

Dave: He's not the only one who forgets.

Jane: What are you talking about?

Dave: You've been known to forget some things.

Jane: Yeah, well, mum's been sitting home alone all afternoon waiting for Fred. He forgot what day it was.

Dave: Looks like you two fell from the same tree.

Jane: What are you talking about?

Dave: You might be interested to know that I got a phone call at the office about half an hour ago.

Jane: So?

Dave: So, do you know what time it is?

Jane: Yeah it's…*[looks at her watch]* Oh no!

Dave: Oh Yes! The headmaster called me. He said our two children had been sitting on the curb for an hour, waiting. Guess who they were waiting for?

Jane: Oh no!

Dave: Oh yes! You forgot our children. Again! I had to leave work.

Jane: I can't believe it!

Dave: Believe it!

Jane: I'm so sorry!

Dave: You certainly are. They're doing their homework, if you care. I've got to go back to the office now. Looks like I'll have to be there till 9:00 tonight to finish preparing for tomorrow's meeting. Don't bother with my dinner. I won't have time for any.

[he exits]

Jane: I can't believe I did it again! How could I forget my own kids? And here I am blaming Fred. Who knows what could have happened? They could have been kidnapped or hit by a car! I can never look the headmaster in the face again! What must that man think of me? I wonder if anyone else saw them out there alone on the curb. Everybody's going to hear about this. All the parents. Everyone in Dave's office. I'll never live it down! We'll have to change schools! How could I be so stupid?

Epilogue
[Each at home, alone]

Fred: What kind of a person forgets her own kids?
Jane: I'm such a rotten mother!
Fred: *I* forgot an *appointment. She* forgot her *children*!
Jane: I hate myself!

Life as we know it!

There is nothing unusual about Fred and Jane. We know them. We can see ourselves in them. Fred and his wife may sit next to us at Sunday worship. Fred may be our son's Scout Leader. Jane might very well turn up at a women's prayer meeting the following morning. Dave works in our office. This is life as we know it: life in the courtroom.

We could say that we find ourselves in this courtroom because a crime has been committed: Fred forgot an appointment with his aged mother. That's true, but a close look at this situation makes it clear that this is no isolated event. It is part of a complex and ongoing pattern. This little series of scenes reveals an orientation, on everyone's part, that is fundamentally legal.

Fred's lapse is viewed as a crime by his sister and him, and it is the crime, not his mother, that becomes the point in what follows. And notice that this stirring up of judgement leads to the rehearsal of many other offences and resentments that bubble to the surface in each person, unbounded by the constraints of timeliness or relevance.

We start with Fred: all his responses to what he has done and to what his sister and his wife say, are self-focused. In Scene I, Fred's personal reflections on his own incompetence and guilt are of no use to his mother. What she needs is his presence and his personally expressed, heart-felt care. But does he go to her, or call? No: he's too busy gathering evidence, making accusations and condemning the guilty (himself). Vitally important things, which have to do with the condition of his heart and the relationships of his life, cry out for attention, but every other possible concern is held hostage to the demands of his primary vocation: judge.

This scene is so common that we might have trouble imagining the alternative! But this incident, involving a forgotten appointment, could have gone another way. The incident alone was just raw material. That "material" could have served other than legal purposes. But what else is there? What would a response look like that is *not* grounded in a legal orientation? After all, Fred *has* failed to follow through on his promise! That's a fact.

But, what if Fred was primarily concerned with loving his mother? What if his orientation is love? What if he is free to judge his behaviour and not himself? He might be free to examine his mind and heart with Jesus to see if there are any unexamined resentments there. Has caring for his mother become just a grim duty? Is there a reluctance to meet with his mother that needs a closer look? It may be a thankless and difficult business, this loving his mother. But he can offer that up to Jesus. After all, Jesus experiences the same thing in loving Fred, so he can be with him in all the temptations that get stirred up as he tries to love his mother. The motivation of love, free from self-judgement, might lead Fred to take seriously the fact that he often has trouble with remembering. Fred might think creatively about things he could do - things that would make it less likely that such a thing would happen again. After all, he wants to grow in his ability to love more effectively and to keep the promises that he makes.

All of this, and many other possible responses, would reflect a commitment to live in the light and the truth; a commitment to deal with habit patterns of sin in his life and to become a person who receives the mercy and love of God so that he can love others as he has been loved. Many "judgements" might be made along the way, but there would be no entry into the destructive judging forbidden in the scriptures.

So the significant thing here is not what Fred *did* in forgetting an appointment. The content - the significance - lies in his *response* to what happened. The content and quality of his response reveals that his orientation is legal. He responds as one who sits on the judgement seat of his own life. The same can be said of the rest of his family. All these scenes take place in courtrooms.

The Courtroom: Whom do we see?

So let's look in the courtroom where Fred and Jane (and their spouses) live. This will not be difficult to picture: we know about courtrooms. It may be that we've "been there and done that", but first-hand experience is not necessary. Much of the world has been flooded with images of the courtroom for several generations through various media. I believe this common familiarity is what the Lord had in mind in bringing the revelation of the courtroom. Most of us can easily picture one and we have a pretty good idea of the kinds of things that go on there, including who the major players are. Let's look at them.

Prologue: lawyers, judges, witnesses, defendants and the like

The prologue begins with the simple discovery that Fred has goofed, but there are hints of what is to come, right from the start. His sister Jane's first few statements escalate from the relatively benign ("You're kidding"), to a reminder that sounds a lot like something being submitted into evidence ("You promised her"). Then we really get going. She issues a statement that leaps much higher up into the legal system ("Well I can believe it! You did the same thing last year … and on her birthday, for heaven's sake!").

What is such an expression? Is it judgement? Well, if one imagines being on the receiving end of a statement like that, one knows that there is more going on than evidence being presented concerning behaviour. Fred has been found guilty of the charge of negligence, and that charge goes beyond a judgement about his behaviour; there are charges being made and judgement being rendered concerning his character (and, ultimately, his identity and worth as a human being): a hint of grievous, perhaps malicious, unreliability! What is more, he is tried again on an earlier charge and convicted of that offence all over again. More evidence is brought out as to the extreme nature of the earlier crime ("And on her birthday, for heaven's sake"). Jane is operating as prosecutor, witness for the prosecution, judge and jury.

But Fred, the defendant, has already pleaded guilty ("I can't believe I did this"). An ominous silence follows. This stirs his sister into taking on another role, very briefly: witness for the defence. She gives evidence supporting a lesser charge: "Well … look, it's not the end of the world. She'll get over it. Really." Jane changes roles because she has become uncomfortable. She senses (chiefly by his silence) that Fred has become his own judge and his own verdict is in. That leads her to offer a very common human counterfeit for love: she tries to make him feel better. But it's not about Fred's feelings really; it's about her own feelings. Jane has become uncomfortable because she identifies with what she knows is going on with Fred. She knows what the silence means: he's stewing in the juice of his own self-judgement. Watching Fred boiling there reminds her (perhaps consciously, but probably unconsciously) of the hell she can make for herself when she sits on the judgement seat of her *own* life. In fact, she's on the fast track to her own legal hell and she'll get there soon enough!

"But you'd better make it up to her." Jane can't let him off too lightly! First of all, he's not innocent, and, second, he might forget that there is another judge that must be dealt with: mum! "Making it up to her" does not mean (for Fred, or for us) that he will be dealing with the truth of what he or his mother may be experiencing; it does not imply action which will reflect or promote relational health; it does not mean an entrance into repentance, forgiveness and reconciliation. All this means is that he must "do his time". The scales of justice must balance. "You'd better make it up to her" means "you'd better serve your sentence: the sentence that will be handed out in her court".

Scene 1: The defendant is the judge

By the time Fred is off the phone, we see that he has moved even more quickly through the legal process than his sister. During the phone silences, it would appear that he has travelled all the way to prison, where a brutal guard (Fred) welcomed the prisoner (Fred) with a good beating. His self condemnation has three major components.

First he curses himself, calling himself names: "stupid … thoughtless … miserable excuse for a son …" Even though he uses some language which may identify his *action* as the offence ("I can't believe I *did* it again") there are several other expressions, and there is the general tone of everything he says, which reveal that his actions are not the main object of his condemnation - he condemns himself as a *person*. Primarily, he curses his *being*: "How can I *be* … I *am* a miserable excuse for a son." *Second*, he grinds himself down by presenting proof that there are no mitigating factors that would lessen his guilt: he was fully aware of his mother's need and of the probable impact of his thoughtlessness. *Third*, he condemns his failure to visit as an expression of ingratitude: "When I think of all she's gone through: She practically died when I was born! Some gratitude this is!"

All this leads to the pronouncement of judgement. First, his sins are unforgivable. "Will she ever forgive me?" is a thinly disguised confession that he cannot imagine ever forgiving himself. Second he judges himself to be unworthy of love: "I hate myself!"

But there is more. Because the world is a courtroom, one person's judgement is woven into mutually reinforcing habit patterns of judgement shared among family and friends. This is certainly evident with Fred, and not just with his wife and Jane. For instance, what are we to make of this: "I can't imagine what she thinks of me. She'll probably give me the silent treatment now." Why would he say this? He says it because he has experienced this form of punishment from his mother. "The silent treatment" is a stock sentence she imposes on folks, like her son, who find themselves convicted of a crime in her court. But there is also this: "When I think of all she's gone through: She practically died when I was born! Some gratitude this is!" There may be some factual basis to this (she may, in fact, have almost died when he was born), but why is it so closely bound up with guilt and punishment in Fred? The answer is simple: her courtroom technique also includes the marshalling of such guilt producing evidence as this: "You can refuse to do this one little thing for me when I carried you for nine months, most of it in a heat wave, and I almost died giving you birth? Some gratitude! You don't even know the meaning of the word!" There is no doubt about it, the judgement in Fred (or in any of us) is not just due to "nature": it has been nurtured, too!

As we have said, Fred's mother, the judge, will need to be given something that she accepts as adequate punishment/payment for the offence (he will have to "make this up" to her). He will have to serve his time or make restitution, etc. But there's not a lot of hope here for any clear cut finish to this. Some judges demand a bribe with the unspoken understanding that if payment is made, the jail time will go away. But one might pay the bribe only to find out that the tables have been turned and extortion is the name of the game: another payment is demanded and more can be anticipated in the future, with no end in sight. In other words, Fred is likely to hear about this for months - even years - no matter how much he "makes it up to her". The record of this conviction will stay on her books forever.

Scene 2: Enough judgement to go around!

Fred's sister seems well aware of her mother's courtroom procedures too. We see this as she first begins to process what has happened: "Oh Lord, it's going to take mum a long time to get over this one." She is aware that mum doesn't quickly move past an offence. What follows is a swamp of smelly resentments, all adding up to one clear judgement: her mother is unjust: "Of course, with mum, Fred can do no wrong. She'll probably find a way to make it my fault. *He* forgets ... but somehow it's *my* fault. She always turns it around. And I end up apologizing because he's a crummy son."

But there is more in this swamp than resentment and judgement about mum. We said at the beginning that as judgement is stirred up in each person, other offences and resentments bubble to the surface, many of which have nothing directly to do with the situation. Usually they function, however, as evidence brought forward to justify the judgement. Jane has judged mum as "unjust". Her verdict is constructed on two pillars. First, she believes her mother judges her brother unjustly ("Of course, with mum, Fred can do no wrong!"). Second, she believes that she, herself, is judged unjustly ("He forgets ... but somehow it's my fault"). Both the verdicts, "innocent" and "guilty", are unjust!

To support the charge that her brother is judged (as innocent) unjustly, Jane brings out all the evidence she can to prove that he's far from innocent - he most certainly *can and does* do wrong. By forgetting the appointment, Fred has sinned against Jane! In fact, he does this routinely ("He's always doing this to me"); Fred doesn't care about anyone but himself ("I don't think he even cares about her. He certainly doesn't care about me. Fred cares about Fred."). He is ungrateful ("The last time I gave him a birthday present he didn't even thank me"). And, finally, she accuses Fred of purposefully ignoring her efforts. It's not just a matter of his not knowing a thing about what she does for her mother: she judges the motives behind this ignorance: he doesn't *want* to know! So much for Fred as the one who can do no wrong.

Now we shift to Jane's case that she has also been judged (as guilty) unjustly - not forgetting that all of this is evidence to justify her judgement of mum as an unjust judge. She must present evidence of her tireless devotion to Fred's mum. The list is long: laundry, bed changing, medicine, food, endurance through weeping. From the lofty judge's "bench", Jane squints down at a Fred who, in contrast with her documented righteousness, can now be simply and summarily dismissed as one who "forgets her birthday". In describing the heights of her devotion, Jane has really gone on a judgement "roll" and all the world is at her feet. There is enough judgement to go all the way around the equator three times and tie a bow. Not only is she the only righteous judge, but from her perch she sees that she is the only one who is righteous *at all*; Jane alone holds all things together, and not only does she get no *help* - she gets no *support*! All should cringe before her, wallowing in guilt; that includes Fred and that "woman he married", and Mum, of course. And that husband of hers? "Forget about it!"

Scene 3: From prison to the bench: so far and yet so near

Meanwhile, back at Fred's house, things make a "U" turn. As his wife, Fran, enters, Fred is obviously continuing his recitation of the guilt producing evidence offered by mum in the courtrooms of many yesterdays. Not only did she almost die giving him birth, but she "worked that rotten job for 12 years just to save money to put [him] through college". The fact that his mother uses the guilt this fact produces for her purposes has been noted by Fran. More than simply *noting* this, she has filed it away as an offence against Fred by his mother ("Yeah and she never lets you forget it"). She "picks up" this offence and becomes his defender. Perhaps because a good offence can be the best defence, mum has been brought up on charges and has been judged. What is the judgement? Perhaps that his mother is a "manipulator" of people. But there are a variety of other judgements that may have been handed down in this daughter-in-law's heart: "Unloving! Unfair! Guilt-tripper!" The list could go on. But, again: it is not behaviour alone about which judgements are

30

being made. It is *Mum herself* who is being judged. This is not a case of "hate the sin, but love the sinner". This is not love in any form. This is the action of the heart to which Jesus refers when he says: "Do not judge."

But we are in the courtroom. And the convicted, sentenced criminal (Fred) is about to become the judge (along, of course, with several other roles such as prosecuting barrister and witness for the prosecution). The turning comes with a nudge from his wife, who, as we said, acts as though an offence is the best defence. After disposing of mum, she goes after the other perceived offender: Jane ("Miss Perfect!"). Fred offers a nice little defence of Jane on the first charge, but then the second charge is made: "When was the last time she remembered your birthday?" This is the old "who's she to talk, she does it too" indictment. Fred makes the mistake of trying to defend her again: "Well she's busy with the kids". This is easy game for the prosecutor, who instantly becomes a hostile character witness. Fran accuses Jane of being a lazy, "soap" watching hypocrite, and then she invites Fred into a one hundred and eighty degree turn! She says in effect: "Everything you've done is understandable and justifiable, and you're not the bad guy here! You have nothing to be sorry about. You're actually the victim! You're the victim of a huge injustice and your sister is the one who ought to be on trial." Fred folds. He gives up defending his sister. It didn't take much - his heart really wasn't in it. In making the turn, Fred doesn't get off the judgement seat, he just swivels in his chair, taking on a more comfortable and satisfying case than his own. He joins his wife in judging Jane ("Yeah. You know what? You're right!").

And so it goes. What follows is typical: evidence is presented to complete the exoneration of the previous defendant (Fred) and more evidence comes in support of the case being made against the new defendant (Jane). Fred, it is alleged, gives more than his sister, who repays his generosity with condemning criticism. Fred goes from the shirker to the sacrificially dutiful and his sister is tossed down from her throne onto that great universal heap of ingrates, cheapskates, do-nothings and hypocrites. In the end, Jane is reduced by the former defendant, with a little deft help from his wife, to a convicted criminal; a pitiable object of mockery: "Unbelievable!"

Scene 4: "And with the measure you use ..."

Jane sits alone with the leftovers of her judgement. Tomorrow, she's going to have to put up with some of the mess her brother made today. But, just as things took a big turn for Fred when a new ingredient was stirred in, the worm turns now for Jane with her husband's entrance.

If you see it coming for Jane, you cringe! How many times have we blamed others for what it turns out we did? How many times have we judged others and found ourselves later being judged for the same thing? How many times have we lived out the fulfilment of Jesus' words: *"For in the same way you judge others, you will be judged, and with the measure you use, it will be measured to you* [Matthew 7:2]"? Enough! We've been there enough that we can understand this scene from the inside. We understand, because we have seen it and lived it, that the more lofty the platform from which we judge, the more devastating the flailing plunge to the rocks below that is sure to follow.

Jane has been way, way up there. But a painful truth is on the way: She and her brother (and all of us) "fell from the same tree"! She has wrapped herself in the robe of a judge but her husband strips it off with a simple question: "Do you know what time it is?" Yes. But she has forgotten what she was supposed to be doing a while ago. Like Fred did. She's just like Fred. This truth is injected deeply: "You forgot your children. Again!" Evidence of her guilt is produced and it points even beyond her neglected children. Because of her, her husband has paid the price of inconvenience, wasted time and hunger.

Dave, after lobbing his guilt grenades, quickly moves on, having other things to do. But she carries on without him, searching out the depths of her guilt and imagining the horrible consequences of her depravity. Not only does she condemn herself for what actually happened - she condemns herself for what *could* have happened ("They could have been kidnapped or hit by a car.") Because she takes the judgement seat and is about to render her verdict, she assumes judgement in the hearts of all others connected with the sordid affair: the headmaster, anyone who might have witnessed her shame, all the parents, her husband's colleagues—all will judge her as she is judging herself. And, as with Fred, it's all about her. What do the children need now? That is not on the agenda. It's probably no big deal to them, but one doubts that would make much difference. They may have only forgiveness and mercy for her, but she is not likely to be able to receive either. There is no place in her for mercy: mercy would be an offence to justice in her courtroom! There is no way out. Jane has arrived where Fred began: in ruthless self-condemnation ("I'm such a rotten mother! ...I hate myself!"). But symmetry is maintained: Fred has arrived where Jane began ("What kind of a person forgets her own kids? *I* forgot an *appointment. She* forgot her *children!*").

The Courtroom: many roles, one agenda.

In American football, "receivers" sometimes run in a pattern called a "crossing route". In the process of running out the play, the player who, in the offensive formation, started on the left end of the "line", ends up on the right side of the field, and the one who started on the right, ends up on the left. As they run down field, they cross in the middle. This is meant to confound the defence whose business is to stop these receivers from catching the ball that is about to be thrown to one of them. That's the way things went with Fred and Jane. But their crossing pattern might be described in more than one way. We might say that Fred started out as a defendant, while Jane started as the judge: they cross midfield and she ends up the defendant and he the judge. There is some accuracy to this description. Certainly on the level of their personal experience, he goes from one who feels guilty and condemned to one who feels himself qualified to judge, though he may have another name for it and may feel completely justified in doing it. She, of course, moves in the opposite direction.

But their subjective feelings or perceptions are not the truth, which comes most fully when we understand the "crossing" in a different way. The fuller truth is that Fred has moved from *judging himself* to *judging his sister*. His sister, having started by judging him, "crosses in the middle" and ends up on the other side, judging herself. So it doesn't matter where they start or end up. In football, the "receiver" is there to *receive,* no matter the particular pattern he runs - that's just meant to confuse and hamstring the defence. Fred and Jane are there, living in the courtroom of this world, sitting on the throne of judgement in their own hearts. Make no mistake, they are there to *judge*, no matter what "role" patterns they run; no matter where they start, or where they end up. Behind the patterns of defence and offence sits a judge who simply turns on the throne he or she occupies, facing first in one direction, then in another.

†

Chapter 3

THE COURTROOM:
from misdemeanour to murder

The Courtroom: A closer look

We know very little about the nature of the judgement we may happen to witness in our daily life. What lies behind the obvious thing we see? Is this mild example only what it appears to be for this person or in this family, or is this the very mild public face of judgement at its most devastating? Is this a "misdemeanour" or "murder"? The truth is that it could be either, or anything in between.

In the course of this book we will look at examples representing the full range of judgement, from what seems to be the most severe to the least. But in many situations it's hard to tell how much destructive power is in force. We would have to see more of the context of these acts of judgement. But, we might ask a more fundamental question: how do we *know* that there is judgement going on at all? The answer is that we don't for *sure* … only God knows the heart. Only he knows who is on the throne. Why do we *suspect* that judgement is there in the examples we consider? Well, for one thing, we have a clue, given by God: *we recognize courtroom activity*!

And let's not forget that we have been told the truth - it's found there in God's word - about how children of the Father behave toward one another as they live out their life in the Father's house. Jesus describes those relationships. So does Paul, Peter, James, John, and so on. We can compare what we see to that standard.

For example, since we are called to love one another as we have been loved by Jesus, we can and should examine our behaviour in the light of what we know love to be. Paul reveals a fundamental aspect of that love: it does not harbour resentment or keep thinking about wrongs that may have been suffered at the hands of others. In other words, love *"keeps no record of wrongs"* [1Corinthians 13:5 NIV]. If we are alert to this truth, we quickly become aware of times when we have begun to accumulate evidence against someone who has offended us. We will know that we have strayed from the ways of love when we hold in bitter remembrance things done long ago. The love that has been poured out within us is not expressed in hearts that take hold of bitterness, accumulate lists of accusations and grasp at evidence to support self-righteous judgements. The cold heart that lifts itself up in such judgement is not the warm place where love has been made flesh. No: the heart where evidence is gathered is the stone altar of an idol.

"True", you might say. "True, but we don't live love out perfectly! I may be falling a bit short today. People in these illustrations may very well be committed to knowing and following Jesus and they may be a lot more loving, in general, than what these isolated examples would indicate. We all 'fall off the wagon!'"

Yes! The context counts and we do not know what any human act "is" in the perfect way that God does. But we do have God's living word as a plumb line. And we do not want to find ourselves making arguments in order to justify the very judging which his word prohibits!

Besides, we are not looking at these illustrations in order to judge the people in the examples! We are looking at behaviour, with

Jesus, so that he can open our minds and hearts to his work in *us*: he wants *us* to be free of destructive judgement in all forms. He wants us to understand the depths of judgement in the human heart. He wants us to know, because he loves us, how devastating *all* "Matthew 7" judgement is: the "misdemeanour" judgement grows on the same tree as the judgement called "murder". And, as we will see in the following chapters, all judgement is nothing less than idolatry. That truth is sobering. If we acknowledge this truth, we cannot ignore the devastation of our idolatry simply because we aren't *always* there serving a false god. If we are "off the wagon", we need God's mercy and forgiveness, not some form of "cheap grace" that we dispense to ourselves.

We turn now to an example that appears to fall within the range of "ordinary and everyday". But is it? Is this a misdemeanour or murder? Well, that depends …

Out shopping in the courtroom

I caught an exchange between a husband and wife recently. The two of them, along with their daughter, were out shopping. Although I suspect the man had just expressed impatience, I don't know for sure what had just happened. I heard him say, "I'm sorry, honey." "Don't give me that", she fired right back, "you couldn't care less about what I want!" Her words dripped as from an overfilled bowl of liquid guilt. As they disappeared down the aisle of the store I heard him say, "Well, I took time *I don't have* out of my *only day off*, didn't I?" His words were delivered in the finely honed tones of unjustly wounded innocence with a couple of mini guilt bombs of his own thrown in, no extra charge ("took the time *I don't have* … my *only* day off").

We cannot know the severity of the judgement that seems to be going on here. But we can sketch out some of the possibilities. It will be instructive to consider possible contexts for this little scene: the larger context of specific acts of judgement can make all the difference in the severity of the consequences of that judgement.

In this example we begin in the common place: with a prosecutor and a defendant. The husband has been brought up on charges. The defendant is accused by the prosecuting barrister of committing certain crimes: first, he is insincere - he doesn't mean what he says; second, he doesn't care about the needs of his wife; this not a misdemeanour, but rather a felony count: he *could not care any less*. didn't hear the evidence presented to support this case, but you may be sure that there was some, which might have been interesting to the teenage daughter who was with them. She was probably a member of the jury whose role is to weigh all evidence and render a verdict.

Dad, the defendant, pleading innocent and acting as his own lawyer, presents the case for the defence. He puts into evidence his costly personal sacrifice to rebut her charge of felony non-caring in the first degree. It should be noted that later, in chambers, he may try to get the charges reduced to a misdemeanour (this was a case, your honour, of "involuntary slippage of an impatient sigh", or some such thing), but for now any such admission would simply weaken his case and would surely be regarded as evidence that could and would be used against him in a court of law.

The problem for the defence is that the verdict is already in. He's guilty. Notice that she's the judge as well as the prosecutor - as we have seen, we wear a stack of hats here in the courtroom - and in cases like this, the prosecutor often continues to gather evidence after the judge's own verdict is in, and, if there's a jury around, they need to be polled. Somewhere down the aisle, following the defendant's statement, mum may have rolled her eyes at her young teenaged juror. Translated, this means, "what say you, members of the jury, guilty, or not guilty?" If the juror purses her lips, shakes her head, then looks heavenward, the verdict is in: "guilty, your honour!"

Legal complications multiply

One might note that the legalities can get very tangled if the jury (the daughter) buys the defence: What if the juror responds with this: "Oh come on, mum! Dad didn't promise to shop all afternoon! You always have trouble making up your mind!" Things would get messy from a legal standpoint. The juror has given a verdict of innocent, but that's pretty hard to do in this case without at the same time taking on the role of "witness for the defence" in order to justify the verdict, which, in our hypothetical, she does. And things being what they are in this kind of court, she ends up judging the case too, dismissing the charges against Dad on the basis of "justifiable impatience".

But this does not exhaust the threads in this legal knot. In this scenario, the daughter has become an barrister, filing charges against the judge (mum) on behalf of her new client (dad)! Mum (the plaintiff/prosecuting barrister/judge) has become a defendant. The first charge is a serious one: the defendant is unreasonable and unjust (an especially serious charge to make against a judge). The defendant is also charged with malicious dawdling. The plaintiff seeks damages: by means of her refusal to make a quicker decision, and through subsequent public slander, the defendant has caused the plaintiff physical discomfort and mental and emotional suffering.

Notice that the new lawyer (namely the daughter, who has been juror, witness for the defence and judge) has also become, in effect, a plaintiff is her own right. Separate charges are being filed. Actually, this may not be a new filing, but evidence in an old case with no statute of limitations. The charge is depraved indifference to the impact of her mum's - the defendant's - actions on the time and patience of others; specifically, a pattern of frequent refusals to make up her mind.

Reflections on the case so far

1. Since she has already judged her husband in her heart, there is no real interest for this wife in being "objective" - we are not observing a search for truth. But there is nothing in the husband's response that would indicate that he is any more interested in searching out the truth. There are signs that both are in the courtroom: neither one can acknowledge any guilt - that would weaken their case and provide legal ammunition for the other side.

2. In my hypothetical, the daughter charged her mother with injustice. If that were the case, it would be likely that this began as the husband's judgement, rendered many times in many ways and passed on to his daughter. His protest of innocence may simply be more evidence offered in the ongoing trial of his wife: "See? There she goes again! This is just one more instance of her unjust treatment of me. I go out of my way to do what she wants, but it's never enough!" Part of the pattern is that he calls on his daughter to support his case. If the wife does the same, the daughter is caught in the middle, constantly being asked to choose between her parents in their ongoing courtroom struggle.

3. When a relationship is, essentially, a court case, that is because each has judged the other. After that, the struggle is over justification: I must defend and justify my verdict and appeal yours. You must do the same. This is the extreme. In most relationships, certainly in ones where the grace of God has entered in and is being received, there may be one or more "cases" going on, but all of it comes in a larger context of openness, vulnerability, truth, genuine repentance and forgiveness, and so on.

Crime and punishment: the sentence

We have yet to consider that following the rendering of a verdict, the guilty are given a sentence. The wife may sentence her husband to one week of arctic wilderness confinement. But the possibilities are endless. Withering looks might follow. In the following days, he might be subjected to pointed comments about the appliance that doesn't work properly, but she's "probably going to have to put up with it forever", because "of course I couldn't possibly ask you to go with me to get a new one … it's too much trouble to bother to spend the time". Or if he asks something of her, she may give him this: "Oh sure, I'll take the time *I don't have* (this in "his voice") to help you when I've got 15 other things I have to do. One good thing though: at least it's not *my only day off* (his voice again)… (here a perfectly timed silence, then:) *I don't get a day off!*" All these are examples of garden-variety "guilt-tripping" as punishment.

Let's remember that the husband is probably living in judgement of his wife. It is vitally important that we keep in mind that these judgements have the same root as hers, in that they began with his subjective experience: in his case, her behaviour toward him. He feels hurt, offended, shamed, degraded, frustrated, and so on. He judges her behaviour as unjust, hurtful, unfair, etc. But it doesn't end there. He ends up judging her *as a person*. It is not just that she *acted* unjustly - she *is* unjust. And there is a fallen world of difference between those two things. He has convicted her of *being* an unjust judge; in his heart, he embraces and pronounces a word concerning her identity. It is nothing less than a curse.

Having judged her *being*, the husband may have some punishing of his own to do. For instance, he may sentence her to three days of wounded silence. Or he could go in the other direction and inflict shame through calculated kindnesses that play on the wife's well-documented tendency, in these cases, to feel humiliation at having been "the bitch in public" yet again. That might not work, though. It might be taken as pathetic, guilty fawning - a blatant and transparent attempt to get her to feel sorry for him and commute his sentence - admissible as yet more evidence that he only cares about himself. He will have to decide whether, in this particular case, it is most effective to heap coals or to dump ice on her head. The better he knows her, the more competent he will be in applying the most effective punishment.

Before we conclude that this is a typical little domestic scene we must acknowledge that the larger context means a lot. This pattern of judgement might come in the context of a basically healthy relationship. They may be aware of this destructive path that they fall into at times and they may be working on it, together to some degree, trying to behave differently. In a rare case they may be looking at the roots of their behaviour together, asking for and receiving forgiveness. They might discover that this destructive path is the result of hurts and resentments that have not been shared and dealt with and which, therefore, function like little exploding time bombs from the past, triggered in the present, but having little to do with it.

On the other hand, what we have described here may be about as good as it gets for this couple. This one incident may be just a mild skirmish in an all out war where no holds are barred and no weapon unused. This may be a fight "to the death". Imagine that this husband has a well of violence in him. What punishment may be coming when they get home? What if the scene went differently after they disappeared down the aisle? What if the husband sees his wife roll her eyes and he says, "What the hell was that?", and there's a threatening edge to his voice? What if the daughter says "Please: she didn't mean anything by it. Let's just forget it", and he grabs his daughter's arm, cutting off the circulation, and stage whispers, "you stay out of this, or you'll see whether we forget about it when we get home!"

We may never have connected something like that tragic human devastation with human judgement. But it's all about judgement. What if, as a boy, the father had been continually, mercilessly judged by his own violent father as a worthless, stupid failure who could never do anything right? What if he saw his mother beaten more than once and heard his father blame him because his "stupid mistake" had "made" the father so angry that he "couldn't help" himself. What if he learns that both the father's anger and his mother's abuse were "his fault". As a grown man he does not need the voice of his father passing vicious judgement on him: he does it himself. He has a deep well of self-contempt, which pours out whenever he hears, or thinks he hears, the message coming at him that he is "not doing it right"; that he is "worthless". Any criticism comes as evidence of his worthlessness. He hears it when it's there; he hears it when it's not there. He hears it everywhere because he carries the judgement with him wherever he goes. He lives under the weight of that judgement and though he reacts violently to it, and despite the fact that he has constructed walls around himself for protection and concealment, it's power comes from the fact that it has become his judgement of himself. He has become exactly like his father.

Judgement in the courtroom: the big picture

We have begun by looking at some symptoms of judgement in terms of the roles we play in the courtroom. I believe that we have seen enough that the "big picture" can begin to come into focus. The *ultimate* consequence of human judgement is estrangement and isolation - the destruction of all human relationships, including the relationship we have with others (both individuals and groups), ourselves, and God

Having looked ahead to the "ends" of judgement, we concentrate now on questions related to its beginnings. How was the "courtroom" built? Where is this fundamental idolatry rooted? What does scripture reveal about the genesis of judgement?

BOOK ONE:
THE COURTROOM

Part Two

Counterfeit Judges:
How We Got Here

†

Chapter 4

THE GENESIS OF JUDGEMENT

Deception & rebellion

Scripture reveals that human bondage to idolatry - specifically to judgement - began in the garden of Eden. There in the garden we were deceived. There we disobeyed. Both are true: the deception and the disobedience. First the serpent seduced humanity through deception. Then in our human, God given will, we rebelled. It is essential that we keep in mind these twin tap roots of "the fall": we were deceived, but the Satanic work of deception was received and given power and dominion in our hearts through wilful disobedience. Our "fall" into idolatry was the result of both a push and a leap!

The Father's provision

In the home which he had given them, God revealed himself to Adam and Eve as their provider. He knew their needs and loved them by caring for them. But the provision that God made for them came in the form of both permission and prohibition. Why? Because not everything in the Garden was good for them. It was as simple as that. The Father could not love them without warning them of harm. "You must not eat from the tree of the knowledge of good and evil, for when you eat of it you will surely die" [Genesis 2:17].

47

We could say that those words of permission and prohibition were God's law and that when Adam and Eve disobeyed, they were breaking the law. But I believe it is important for our understanding of both our "fall" and our salvation that we consider the events of the Garden of Eden through relational eyes. Our personal identity, our provision and our purpose as human beings, were to be centred in, and dependent upon, our relationship with God. From this perspective, we see there was no law in the garden. There was just a father and his children. This is how it was intended for us by God in creation. When a father tells his children what he wants them to do and what he wants them not to do, his words are not a legal document in verbal form. It's just that a father loves his children. He provides them with good things and warns them of harm. His children don't obey out of solemn respect for the law and the fear of punishment. No. His children love their daddy. And they trust him. They trust him without limit or reservation with clean, soft, open hearts. Just as their daddy's word was an expression of his love, their trusting, obedient response is simply their love offered in return. Is this not, precisely the relationship Jesus had with his Abba?

We were created for this love relationship of child-like trust. And it was this relationship, which was life itself for Adam and Eve, that the serpent sought to undermine and destroy in the garden.

The serpent's wedge

In his very first words to Eve, the serpent sets in motion his plan of distortion, deception and alienation. *"Did God really say 'you must not eat of any tree in the garden?"* The serpent did not initiate this conversation for the purpose of helping Eve to come closer to God. Eve was not being invited to identify more clearly the path of obedient love. This conversation is not about doing God's will: it is about finding a way around his will. The serpent begins by inviting

Eve into a conversation *about* God. Eve is not talking *with* God. She's not talking *to* God. She is having this conversation *apart from* her relationship with God the Father. And, as far as the deceiver's purposes go, that is the point.

We are witnessing an occult crash course: *"How to come out from the bondage of your identity as a child of God to a new one of your choosing; one where you get to be like God.* This is a long title for a crash course, but very seductive, especially the part about getting to be like God.

The deceiver delivers his message. It is the same now as it was then: "This is the God", he says, "who told you what to eat and what not to eat, but who never bothered to inform you concerning your options. Isn't there something suspicious about someone who gives you an order and doesn't explain it; who doesn't ask you your opinion? There must be something he's hiding. Apparently you're supposed to just accept this without question. But there's no way to know if what he says is really true or not. In fact, I'm telling you right now that he wasn't telling you the truth when he said you would die. You'll go on breathing and God knows it."

In all of this, the serpent is using deception to drive a wedge between God's children and God. He seeks to destroy that relationship by attacking its foundation, which is child-like trust and responsive love expressed as obedience. Their creator's love has been expressed to them in his word of loving provision, both permissive and prohibitive. But notice: God's will has ceased to be a given. This is critical. In the mouth of a liar, God's will has been presented as an option.

God's will: an option

Think of it. Consider the battle in our own hearts. Even in those of us who seek to follow Jesus Christ and do the will of the

Father; we who are born again (from above) by the Holy Spirit [John 3:3, 5] - even in us this battle still goes on, doesn't it? The way of Adam still opens up before us. We say, "I believe this is God's will! But... on the other hand, it's not so simple; there are things that need to be considered. Did God really say that? And if he said it, what did he mean by it?" The bottom line is this: God's will is an option that we as Christians take *very seriously*! Sometimes we choose that option. Sometimes we don't. This is fundamental to the fallen human condition. It is an orientation which persists in our lives as Christians.

So Eve is invited to consider the options. The serpent says, in effect, "you can leave this tree alone, as God said. That's an option. But, there's another way of looking at this. God formed Adam and you with his own hands and put you in charge here on earth and gave you this kingdom to rule over and care for. Shouldn't you be the ones to decide what's best? Don't worry about the 'dying' thing: if you eat from this tree you won't be dead! Really! You'll just have knowledge, that's all. You'll be like God in knowing good and evil. You'll be much better equipped to do the job you've been given to do! How can you *not* want knowledge? Are you really going to choose ignorance?"

Choices: True and False

The choice: not ignorance, but trust

This is very important: we have inherited that question! Is that what you choose as a Christian: to remain ignorant? That is the question asked by the prince of this world. That is even what the Church asks when it embraces the things of the kingdom of this world and takes those things into its life. As a current example we hear this: "Don't listen to all those poor ignorant people down there in the global south who actually believe all that primitive stuff in that Bible we gave them. Leave behind the ancient ignorance and take hold of the new wisdom." The choice, says Satan, is between knowledge and ignorance.

There is just one problem: Satan is a liar. The true choice was not between knowledge and ignorance. In the garden, the serpent deceived Adam and Eve into thinking that they were children of ignorance. But they were children of God their Father. The choice to obey would not have been a choice to go on in ignorance. It would have been a choice to go on living with and from God in child-like trust.

The serpent pulled the wool over their eyes by convincing them that eating of the tree of the knowledge of good and evil meant that their eyes would be opened and they'd look around in the world and suddenly they'd see and know for the first time! The assumption is that they don't know what is good *now*, but they will *then* - they can't see what is evil *now*, but they will see it and recognize it *then*. That lie was like a knife twisted into the hearts and minds of the Father's children. They were deceived *and* in their pride they wilfully rebelled, looking away from the simple life giving truth.

The truth was that Adam and Eve were not ignorant. They already knew what was good and what was evil. They had been told, in person, by God: "This is good for you. This is not."

They knew everything they needed to know about good and evil concerning the choice they were being tempted to make about the eating of fruit. But the deceiver succeeded in diverting their eyes from the choice itself to some imagined future benefit. Dazzled by a lie about the benefits of forbidden fruit, Adam and Eve were no longer content to know only what the Father wanted them to know and to trust him for the rest. So they turned away; not from ignorance, but from trust; not from an idea, but from a relationship.

The choice: not seeing, but judging

To repeat: "... the serpent succeeded in diverting their eyes from the choice itself to some imagined future benefit." This final deception involved another absolutely critical assumption: that the only things at issue for Adam and Eve were the things that were to happen *after* they ate the fruit: namely that their eyes would be opened and that they would be like God in "knowing good and evil". But while it is true that sin and death entered into the world with the eating of the forbidden fruit, *the door of Sin and death was opened by Adam and Eve through their choice to eat the fruit. That choice was nothing less than a wilful decision to stand in God's place as judge.*

The serpent's most devastating deception came in what he did *not* say: he failed to mention that *before they could eat they would have to judge*. God pronounced the fruit evil for them, but they overturned his righteous judgement and pronounced it good [Genesis 3:6]. That was the turning, and the *over*turning of their life as the children of God. They didn't know what they were doing; they didn't consciously decide to go off the deep end: they were pushed. But it was more than deception. They also disobeyed. They wanted what they wanted. They chose to leap. Wilful rebellion worked hand in glove with deception and Adam and Eve took God's throne of judgement in their own hearts. They took their lives in their own hands. They became judges of the law [James 4:11f], and in judging they were judged.

Judgements of Counterfeit Judges

Then, as newly minted judges, they render their second ruling. They pronounce their bodies shameful. At this point when they look at themselves they see with judging eyes and they speak from the overflow of rebellious, judging, guilty hearts, and they call evil what God has called good. They think they see, but they have become blind to the truth.

It's worth noting that at this point Adam and Eve have taken on a new identity: "guilty, shameful, rebellious Judge". This is the inheritance they now pass on. Things are just as God said they would be: they have turned from life and chosen the way of death; they are spiritually dead and, soon enough, they will be physically dead.

So Adam and Eve, dead but still breathing, go hide from God. They are judges hiding behind a tree. (Great huge sin and guilt hiding behind a skinny little tree.) And they start conspiring to place the blame, because that is what judges do.

They are in desperate need of mercy, but they have placed themselves in their own hands and those hands hold no mercy, only judgement. True mercy can only come from the true Judge: the one with all power and authority. The mercy they need can only come from the one who *is* mercy.

So, in the attempt to justify themselves they make a third judgement. They judge themselves as innocent. "It's not my fault. She did it." "No, he did it." It is no use: none of their judgements are going to help. Certainly not this one. The human verdict of "innocent" - as much a judgement as "guilty" - is just a useless counterfeit of God's mercy. First, it's a lie and everyone knows it, including the liars. Second, it cannot take the place of the Father's love. Third, it cannot give them back the life they have rejected.

So there they sit on God's judgement seat: lost, broken, sinful, prideful, arrogant, deceived and in bondage. They are much too small for this throne; their feet don't reach the floor, or even come near the front edge of the seat.

The State of Things

They sit as incompetents, judging now in genuine ignorance. So do we.

They sit as hypocrites, judging the speck in their brother's eye. So do we.

They sit as idols on the throne in the courtroom of this world. And we've been sitting there in that courtroom ever since.

They sit in need of a Saviour; a Saviour who will come as judge and set them free. So do we. We need the only righteous judge to come and take his place on the judgement seat of our hearts. We need to be saturated with the love and mercy of the One who has come with all power and all authority, not to judge us (to what purpose? if we are on his throne we sit condemned already!), but to save us.

Most of all, Adam and Eve sit there on the judgement seat of their hearts in desperate need of the power to get down off the seat and sit at the feet of the only righteous judge; the power to be their Father's children again. So do we.

†

Chapter 5

"DO NOT JUDGE":
Echoes from the Garden

The scriptural witness

Witness to the devastating consequences of sinful human judging is there to be seen throughout the scriptures, but it comes into sharp, personally challenging focus in the teaching and exhortation of the New Testament (with the coming of the "Righteous Judge"?!). We will concentrate our attention there.

There are two prominent threads to the New Testament revelation about judgement. On the one hand, the people are warned not to judge, and, on the other, there are strong, frequent reminders that God alone is the true judge, with all authority, wisdom, righteousness and power. So far as the exhortation goes, to state the obvious, this word of warning about judging is given to the people *because they need it*. The intensity of these exhortations, not to mention their specific content, allows no other conclusion. One does not ask someone to stop doing something unless they are doing it in the first place [Romans 14:13]! This is not a uniquely Christian disease: Jesus spoke forcefully about the judgement he observed among the Jews just as Paul and James respond in no uncertain terms to the destructive judgement they observe among the members, both Jew and Gentile, of the Christian communities they oversee.

Three reasons are given in scripture as to why we are not to judge one another. It will be useful to look at each one. But first it should be noted that though there are three scriptural reasons, the first two don't count! We'll look at that later. Here we go:

First: we're lousy at it!

Because we are blind

We start with Jesus' words as recorded in Matthew:
How can you say to your brother, 'Let me take the speck out of your eye,' when all the time there is a plank in your own eye? You hypocrite, first take the plank out of your own eye, and then you will see clearly to remove the speck from your brother's eye. [Matthew 7:4ff]

One basic problem is that we don't see very well. When I judge you, my judgement has more to do with my defective organs of perception than with you. The unexamined thing in me blinds me to the truth of you.

We are like the little girl being sent to her room for a "time out" who screams at her mother, "You're a stupid mother and I hate you!" The judgement of her mother as a stupid person is clouded by her anger. So is her judgement of herself as one who hates her mother. She can't see a thing right now.

The same thing happens with adults, of course. For example: let's say that as one adult to another - as your friend - I express concern about your health because you are overweight. You react by saying that you knew all along that I wasn't really your friend; that I was a hypocrite and had been judging you all along while pretending to like you; that I hate fat people; that I'm not mature enough to be a real friend, because I only see the surface and don't take the time or care enough to look deeper and see the real person. Veins are popping. You storm off. Later you share your judgement of me with a few others who become very offended for you and who begin to judge everything I say and do in the light of that offence.

It may be that like the little girl you are not seeing clearly. If you were you would see the truth that your parents were two bitter people who found no joy or meaning in life and who hated "fat people" among many other groups they identified as objects of contempt. This was a pet subject all your young life: "fat people are stupid; fat people are boring; fat people are disgusting". After contact with such a person, the family typically debriefed by sharing all the disgust each one had experienced separately during the contact. Jokes and contemptuous commentary followed. You took this in with mother's milk. Then you grew up. For a variety of reasons you find yourself very much on the heavy side. You've been exposed to more enlightened ideas about the people you used to despise, and you espouse them heatedly, but the judgement runs deeper. The truth is that you hate yourself for being fat. Your judgement of me as a person who judges you is simply *your* judgement of you misdirected! You look out through a plank filled eye and see a plank!

Because we are ignorant

We are poor judges because we are blinded by the plank in our own eye. But we also judge in ignorance - without vital information concerning the human heart. This is significant. Destructive judgement characteristically involves a judgement of the motives of the heart and we do our judging without adequate knowledge concerning the conditions of anyone's heart. Unlike God, as human beings we do not have the capacity to know those things which are hidden there [1 Corinthians 4:5]. I am ignorant concerning the truth of your motives and inner attitudes. I know only a tiny bit, at best, about your past - where your life has been, what you have had to deal with, even if I know the externals. I only see what is apparent and not all that much of that. And I know nothing about the things that cannot be seen, like the tender shoots of change that may be there growing beneath your surface.

It cannot be said of us that our discernment is *"living and active. Sharper than any double-edged sword."* It does not penetrate *"even to dividing soul and spirit, joints and marrow"*. Although we continually judge *"the thoughts and attitudes of the heart"*, it cannot be said that *"Nothing in all creation is hidden from [our] sight"*, or that *"everything is uncovered and laid bare before [our] eyes"*. This penetrating and perfect discernment is attributable to no human being, but only to the word of God [Hebrews 4:12ff]. That doesn't stop us, however. We don't allow ignorance to get in our way. When we enter into judgement, something rises up in us with idolatrous power and we make false claims and we act … well, we act like God. But we're not. What are we? We are judges without information or wisdom.

When the Lord describes, through Isaiah, the one who is to come, The Righteous Branch of Jesse, he describes one who will see past the surface; whose capacity to judge will be rooted in a discernment of truth that far transcends what can be known sensually:

> *"...and he will delight in the fear of the LORD. He will not judge by what he sees with his eyes, or decide by what he hears with his ears; but with righteousness he will judge the needy, with justice he will give decisions for the poor of the earth."* [Isaiah 11:3ff]

Because we are sinful

The judgements of this "Righteous" judge are fully informed by God's truth. His judgements are made within the context of God's word, in obedience and conformity to his will. Therefore, the righteousness and justice which characterize his judgements stand in sharp contrast to ours. We deal out judgements that amount to nothing more than slander [James 4:11]. Slander is not a mistake we make due to a lack of information. It is a tactic we employ to serve our need to control. We do not deal in pure justice, through an obedience fully informed by divinely revealed truth. Instead we render judgements infected with the evil that is in the minds that conceive them [James 2:4], measuring all things by merely human standards [John 8:15]. Basing things on appearances alone, we are too often attuned to shadows of things and not the reality [John 7:24; Colossians 2:16f].

Our judgements flow from our hearts and reflect the stubbornness and lack of repentance found there [Matthew 12:33-37; Romans 2:5]. How can we be anything but corrupt judges? Every time we judge we demonstrate that we belong on the other side of the bench [James 4:11]!

Second: We do the same thing!

Because no one is righteous

Paul saw clearly into the legal orientation of the kingdom of this world. Apparently he had plenty of experience with it, seeing it practiced among Christians, Jews and Gentiles. There are a number of examples recorded in his letters and in Acts where he responds to instances of human judgement by observing that the judgement he sees is occurring in spite of the fact that the one judging is *doing the same thing!*" This was the basis of his challenge to Peter at Antioch

[Galatians 2:11-14]. In this passage he uses the term "hypocrite" which often means "you do the same thing". (When Jesus uses the term "hypocrite" in the passage quoted earlier [Matthew 7:5], it has this flavour and reveals another layer of meaning to his teaching about the evils of human judging. Reasons #1 and #2 are both there, in a few words: they are blind *and* they do the same thing!)

An instructive example from Paul's life is recorded in Acts. After his arrest in Jerusalem, at the end of his discourse before the Sanhedrin, Paul says something which particularly offends Ananias, the high priest: "My brothers, I have fulfilled my duty to God in all good conscience to this day." This is not to be borne! If it is true - if what he has done has been true obedience to God's will - then everyone is going to have to profess faith in Jesus Christ, close up shop and go home!. Paul *must* be a blasphemer, or their world is turned upside down. Ananias has the "blasphemer" struck in the face. Paul does not suffer this in silence:

> *"Then Paul said to him, "God will strike you, you whitewashed wall! You sit there to judge me according to the law, yet you yourself violate the law by commanding that I be struck!"* [Acts 23:3]

"Whitewashed wall!" Translation: "hypocrite". How can this man presume to judge Paul if he is a law breaker himself? In other words: "you do the same thing". But Paul has a problem:

> *"Those who were standing near Paul said, "You dare to insult God's high priest?" Paul replied, "Brothers, I did not realize that he was the high priest; for it is written: 'Do not speak evil about the ruler of your people.'"* [Acts 23:4-5]

Paul seems to have passed judgement upon a man in public without all the necessary information. Does Paul find himself in the position of being an illustration of "reason #1"? Not really. It's just that through ignorance he has acted unwisely. If only he had known, he implies, he wouldn't have said what he said out loud! But Paul did proclaim the truth to the Sanhedrin: the world *had* been turned upside down. The Sanhedrin's judgement of the word of God was not made in ignorance; they had heard the truth. Our dear brother Paul was in good company in receiving the blows of a rebellious world on his way to the cross.

No not one!

"You, therefore, have no excuse, you who pass judgement on someone else, for at whatever point you judge the other, you are condemning yourself, because you who pass judgement do the same things. Now we know that God's judgement against those who do such things is based on truth. So when you, a mere man, pass judgement on them and yet do the same things, do you think you will escape God's judgement? Or do you show contempt for the riches of his kindness, tolerance and patience, not realizing that God's kindness leads you toward repentance."
[Romans 2:1-4]

This passage follows Paul's description of the wretched, depraved condition of a humanity which has turned from the knowledge of God. Now, Paul addresses himself to any Jew who would assume, because he has been given God's law and is one of God's chosen people, that he does not need God's saving grace. He reaches out and grabs them by the front of their robes and shakes them out of their sleep: "You do the same thing! Listen to me: you-do-the-same-thing! Yes, you have knowledge of the truth: don't use it to judge the Gentiles, use it as motivation to repent!".

Paul goes on to describe specific offences, culminating in the devastating point that circumcision means nothing apart from an obedience which comes from the heart [Romans 2:25-29]. We've arrived at the heart. This is good as it is the root of the problem. It is the seat of judgement and its universal condition is the great leveller: *"Jews and Gentiles alike are all under sin... there is no one righteous, not even one ..."* [3:9ff]. Paul's point must not be lost in the specific charges mentioned. His admonishment, "You who pass judgement do the same things", applies whether or not we have done any *particular* "same thing"! It is the act of passing judgement on another person which is the problem. It is the condition of the heart from which the judgement proceeds that is the problem. The judgement *itself* is lawlessness. One criminal cannot justly or righteously judge another criminal. In doing that, one mocks law while ostensibly serving it.

The Garden (an echo)

"Brothers, do not slander one another. Anyone who speaks against his brother or judges him speaks against the law and judges it. When you judge the law, you are not keeping it, but sitting in judgement on it. There is only one Lawgiver and Judge, the one who is able to save and destroy. But you - who are you to judge your neighbour? [James 4:11ff]

Here James describes something which began with our rebellion in the Garden of Eden. There, as we have said, we chose to "be like God" - to be the ones who would judge good and evil. We took the judgement seat. In our own hearts, we became the judge of all things, including God's law. James sees very clearly: we have become counterfeits of both the true Judge and the true Lawgiver.

We make *use* of God's law if it can serve our purposes, but, having become a law unto ourselves, our judgements flow from lawless hearts. We judge not in service of justice and truth but in service of what, at any given moment, seems right "in our own eyes". And, as we know, that is a pathetic situation since, on the one hand, we are blind, ignorant and sinful, and, on the other, we have no perspective or position that would allow us to make judgements, since we are there in the same box, on the same level with the one we are judging!

Who are you?

"Who are you to judge your neighbour?" The answer is, of course, "I am no one to judge my neighbour! I'm lousy at it and I do the same thing. Plus, in order to judge, I would have to have the authority - I would have to be qualified and have higher standing, at least within the legal system, than the person I'm judging. A judge can't take the bench when she herself is under indictment! I think and behave as though I have all the necessary standing when I judge you, but I'm a counterfeit judge. I'm a rebel and I'm deceived. My standing is the same as yours: we are both in the jurisdiction of the only true Judge. I'm not subject to you and you're not subject to me. We are both human beings subject to the one whose word judges all things. He is the only one with the power to judge because he is the only one 'who is able to save and destroy'. Me? I was created by the same God who created you. We are both his fallen creatures. I'm going to die, just as you are. We're both going to have to come before the judgement seat of the one who actually is the Judge."

> *"You, then, why do you judge your brother? Or why do you look down on your brother? For we will all stand before God's judgement seat. It is written:*
>
> *"'As surely as I live,' says the Lord,*
> *'every knee will bow before me;*
> *every tongue will confess to God.'"*
>
> *So then, each of us will give an account of himself to God. Therefore let us stop passing judgement on one another..."* [Romans 14:10-13]

Third: We're not the Judge!

The first two don't count!

Now we have come to it. This is as far as it goes concerning the prohibition of destructive human judgement - this is the clincher; the trump card. This last reason for not judging is *reason enough!* In fact, because we are not the judge, the other two reasons don't count. Not that they are false in any way. On the contrary, they describe the way it is with us as judges. And they can be useful to keep in mind. But they can never stand alone. In the human heart they can cut both ways.

On the positive side, the first two reasons bring awareness of truth which can function to call us back from the brink of acting in judgement - they can help us walk a new way.

But they can be (and are!) used as instruments of our rebellion, actually buttressing the foundations of our judging hearts, justifying our verdicts and the gathering of our evidence, serving our deception. Let's look at the first two reasons again, from this perspective.

I may judge because I see and I know?

Let's suppose that I am pretty aware of the pitfalls of judgement, in that I accept my inability to know the disposition of the heart, or the true motivation of another person. I'm aware of the problem, of its "genesis" and the scriptural prohibition. Even for me, there may still be times when people do things right before my eyes and it's hard to make a case that I'm blind or ignorant.

My boss implied that a raise and a promotion would follow if I took that thankless assignment. But it turns out that he was just using me to motivate another person he was intent on advancing all along. After his strategy works, he fires me with lame justification and noticeable contempt. As I leave the building with all my things, I hear the boss with his newly promoted flunky laughing in his office. I hear my name. I enter into judgement. Now, it may be that I don't see clearly, but I don't believe it. I see *enough*!

Note that a non-judging (or rightly judging!) response may involve the recognition that all is not acceptable here. It may even be our duty to hold one another accountable for actions such as this. There is a wide range of personal responses possible: I might speak truth to this person; make his actions known to those he reports to; I may even seek legal redress. When I act as this man's judge in the way that is prohibited, however, I open myself to destruction. Typical responses arising from such judgement can range from the digging and filling of a well of bitterness that I drink from for years and which poisons my life, to my purchase of a semi-automatic weapon in preparation for my follow up visit to his office.

Let us look at another case. Some years ago a woman was found to have taken the lives of her children. I do not remember the details, but I remember the reaction of a particular person in the church I was serving at the time. It went something like this: "She's an animal. And don't try to tell me we're supposed to forgive somebody like that. I would never, ever forgive her. The very idea disgusts me. They ought to string her up on television." There was more than a hint, in this response, that judging her was not only his right, but that it would have been an obscenity *not* to judge her. He spoke as one who viewed her actions as a violation of the rules of *his* court. She had sinned against him and so came under his jurisdiction (he is "just like God"!). It was his duty to judge her.

And judge her he did. True: his was a response to an act that can only be described as evil working through human agency to accomplish appallingly evil ends. But we must not allow that fact to obscure the nature and depths of the destruction embodied in the response itself. This person was not just making judgements about that mother's behaviour based upon God's law, or acknowledging that consequences must follow. The response was nothing less than an expression of contempt for her very life and a judgement of the eternal disposition of her soul. That churchman responded to an act of murder by condemning the woman to hell and then murdering her in his heart. This act of judgement was literally horrific to witness. *And the strength of the hold this judgement had in the heart of this judge was greatly increased by the fact that he thought he could see and he thought he knew.*

I may judge because it's me with me?

What about the case where judgement enters into a different arena of human relationship where it really does appear that I have all the information needed to judge. What about when I judge myself? There I do not lack information about the case. Though I may not know perfectly, I know well enough. When I use words, I know what they mean. There is no problem with misunderstanding; no mistake in translation when it's me. I felt it and I know I felt it. I thought it, and intended it. I knew what I was doing, and did it anyway. Don't tell me that the plank in my eye is blinding me! *The plank in my eye is the very thing I'm looking at!* No excuse. No lack of seeing or knowing: I'm guilty.

Up to this point, it is possible that all we have described so far in this example is the temptation to judge, not judgement itself. In fact, based on just this much, we might be describing the workings of my God-given conscience. I am brought, by the convicting work of the Holy Spirit, to an awareness of the truth of my sin and, hopefully, to a genuine and necessary sorrow about that. The purpose of this Godly conviction is to lead me to a confession of my sin, true repentance, and the reconciliation that comes through the merciful forgiveness of God - all part of a faithful response to Jesus' call to "remove the plank" from my own eye.

But this doesn't always happen. If I have no acquaintance with or openness to the mercy of the Father, it never happens. What happens instead? I go through all the steps described above, but apart from God. I operate fully in the courtroom, where I sit as judge of my life. *I* convict and condemn *myself. I* sentence *myself* and exact punishment, demanding payment until every last cent of the debt is paid. In some cases I may remind myself of my crime and rehearse the condemnation again and again as punishment. In the extreme case, my judgement may be so severe that I take my own life in an attempt to make the punishment fit the crime.

I have ministered to many Christians who have entered into this self judgement in spite of the fact that they had gone through steps of confession, repentance, etc. Many have said that, at the time, they experienced God's forgiveness, to some degree at least. Most, if not all, would say that they believe God has forgiven them. But here is the thing: they are living under their own judgement, having said, in effect, "God may forgive me, but I never will"! In the hearts of these people, God's mercy is overturned; not fully received. The judge inside knows they don't "deserve" forgiveness. But "deserving forgiveness" is a spiritual oxymoron, typical of the warped reasoning of a counterfeit judge! What's happening is that the judge inside is offended by mercy because it is a miscarriage of justice [see Jonah 4]. The judge is not going to get forgiveness in his or her own court. Forgiveness has no place in the legal system. The debt has to be paid in full. In this courtroom, even when you are released from prison, there is no forgiveness; no full release. Though you've done your time, your sin remains on your record forever.

The point of all this? When I judge myself, much of its power comes from my unshakable belief, so basic that it is assumed, that my judgement is true and just, because I see and I know all that I need to. After all: it's me, myself and I! I may judge because I do not do the same thing?

We have seen that whenever we enter into judgement of another person, we are, in truth, unjustified because we "do the same thing". A sinner can know what is sinful and can recognize it in themselves and others, because God has revealed to us what is good and what is evil. God has made known to us his righteous expectations regarding human behaviour. But the creature cannot justly judge the creature. We can never dole out justice from the well of our own righteousness. We don't have any righteousness we can call our own that's worth the paper it's printed on. However, the perspective that comes from this truth is not what we live with most of the time. We are only aware of what is right there in front of our face. Every day we see or hear about what people do and we enter into judgement because we haven't done it: *we don't do the same thing.* We can see this justification in operation from its weakest, most borderline application, to the most blatant.

"You just lied to me and I judge you in my heart as a liar. Yes I've lied, but that was forgiven and forgotten and that was then, but this is now, and I'm not lying now like you are! Besides when I lied I was frightened. There's no excuse for you! This is just malicious. I make mistakes but I'm not cruel like this. I lie sometimes, but you *are* a liar!" This is pretty thin! But we manage to hide behind it. From ourselves, at least.

Here is a more difficult example: If I hear that someone has stolen money from a old couple, or I read of a rape in the park, it is obvious to me that I do not do these things. If I enter into "Matthew 7" judgement of those people, I am less apt to reflect on that judgement, or even see it *as* judgement, precisely because I so obviously do not do the same thing.

Of course, if I look closer, I may see that if I cheat on my income tax I might, in effect, be stealing from others. And I may be aware that Jesus says that I am committing adultery in my heart if I lust after my neighbour's wife [Matthew 5:27], but I can get past that, and do, almost all the time. "Jesus says contempt is murder too. But it's not really the same. Jesus was just exaggerating to make a point when he says I could go to hell for calling you a fool [Matthew 5:22]. You tell me: if I judge someone to be the worst kind of fool and say so, and dismiss her as a human being, is that the same as stabbing her in the back? It's not. I'll tell you what: I'd rather have you call me a fool than stab me in the back, thank you very much! I don't stab people in the back!" And the gavel hammers down.

There is no doubt about it; reason number 2 is not much of a deterrent for me. I see it can apply to others - and to me once in a while - but most of the time I simply don't believe it. Why don't I believe it? Because I'm convinced that *I don't do the same thing*!

The one that counts!

Reasons No.1 and No.2 fall prey quite easily to the blinding, deceiving nature of human bondage to judgement. But there is a deeper problem. We have been skirting around this problem and it's time to look it in the eye. If those were the only reasons why God did not want us to judge, then the implication is that if somehow they did not apply in a particular situation, we could rightly and justly enter into judgement of a fellow human being, ourselves and God. But they are not the only reasons given in scripture. In fact, they are not so much reasons for not judging as they are descriptions of the kind of judges we are. We're blind, hypocritical judges! But the real reason why I am not to judge is *not* that I am a blind hypocrite. It is that I am not the judge. *"There is only one Lawgiver and Judge, the one who is able to save and destroy. But you - who are you to judge your neighbour."* [James 4:12] This is reason number 3, in the inspired words of James. This is the only one that counts and it is the only one we need: we are not to judge because human judgement of another human being is an illegitimate enterprise, no matter what you see, or know, or do, or don't do.

The only way we can understand the deep well of devastation we tap into when we enter into destructive judgement of another human being, is through understanding the origin of sinful human judging. Human judging is not devastation because we are no good at it. As we have seen in the "Genesis of judgement", human judging is devastation because it is idolatry - the fruit of our rebellion in the Garden of Eden. When, in Adam, we took God's place on the judgement seat of our lives, that idolatrous choice came under the judgement of the word of God. Our judging remains under judgement. So when Jesus says, *"Do not judge"* [Matthew 7:1], he means, "Do not judge when you are blind *and* when you have the eyes of a hawk. Do not judge when you are ignorant *and* when you've got all the facts by the tail. Do not judge when you stand guilty and when you stand all squeaky clean. Do not Judge *or you too will be judged.*" God has judged, is judging and will judge our judgement of other human beings. Why? Because he *is* the Judge! And we're not.

The God who is God!

Paul said it: *"We all stand before God's judgement seat* [Romans 14:10].*"* It doesn't matter what we believe. We can go on thinking and acting like a judge, but when we die, we will meet the God who *is* judge. The Sovereign Lord has allowed the rebellion, but its days are numbered: *"For he has set a day when he will judge the world with justice"* [Acts 17:31]; *"for a time is coming when all who are in their graves will hear his voice and come out - those who have done good will rise to live, and those who have done evil will rise to be condemned* [John 5:28f].*"* All counterfeit judges will be exposed: *"For we know him who said, 'It is mine to avenge; I will repay,' and again, 'The Lord will judge his people.' It is a dreadful thing to fall into the hands of the living God* [Hebrews 10:30f].*"*

It does not matter whether it is good news (*"Now there is in store for me the crown of righteousness, which the Lord, the righteous Judge, will award to me on that day"* [2 Timothy 4:8]), or bad news (*"...he must not be a recent convert, or he may become conceited and fall under the same judgement as the devil."* [1 Timothy 3:6]), it will be the Living God, the only righteous Judge, who delivers it.

And his judgements will not be like ours:

> *"Let them sing before the LORD,*
> *for he comes to judge the earth.*

He will judge the world in righteousness
and the peoples with equity. [Psalm 98:9]

Besides the fact that he is the only and living God, possessing perfect wisdom and power to judge righteously, the Lord has the authority, in the sense of the "right", to judge us. After all *"It is he who made us and we are his ..."* [Psalm 100:3] We belong to him. David, who had reason to know God's just judgements, had it exactly right:

> *"Against you, you only, have I sinned*
> *and done what is evil in your sight,*
> *so that you are proved right when you speak*
> *and justified when you judge ..."* [Psalm 51:4]

Because we are all subject to the true God, we are all under the jurisdiction of the true judge. When we sin by breaking his law, we sin against *him*, not the judging bystanders. This was the reason why the Pharisees and the teachers of the law were offended when Jesus forgave the sins of the paralytic in their presence. After all, *"Who can forgive sins but God alone."* [Luke 5:21]

Ultimately, when we violate the relationship we have with the one who is sovereign through the sin of idolatry it is, first and foremost, the life we have in him that is lost. And only through his mercy can it be restored: *"It is by grace you have been saved, through faith ... for we are God's workmanship ..."* [Ephesians 2:8,10]

The one who *will* judge!

> *"For we must all appear before the judgement seat of Christ, that each one may receive what is due him for the things done while in the body, whether good or bad."* [2 Corinthians 5:10]

The one who will judge us is the one who saves us: Jesus Christ. He will judge *"the living and the dead* [Acts 10:42]*."* He will judge as the *"Son of Man"* [John 5:27], as the Word of God [Hebrews 4:12f] and as the *"Alpha and the Omega"*, who, when he comes on the last day, *"will give to everyone according to what he has done* [Revelation 22:12f]*."* Our Lord Jesus will judge us in glory, power and majesty, because the Father ...

> *"...exalted him to the highest place and gave him the name that is above every name, that at the name of Jesus every knee should bow, in heaven and on earth and under the earth, and every tongue confess that Jesus Christ is Lord, to the glory of God the Father."* [Philippians 2:9-11]

The one who *is* Judge!

But though Jesus Christ will be on the judgement seat on the last day, it is not his seat [Romans 14:10]. He will do the judging, but, ultimately, he is not the Judge. And in the glorious mystery of his economy, the Father, who *is* the Judge, will do no judging [John 5:22]! Not directly. He shares everything with his Son. The sovereign Lord accomplishes his purposes through his Beloved.

God the Father is the Judge. Jesus witnessed to this truth in his earthly ministry: *"I am not seeking glory for myself; but there is one who seeks it, and he is the Judge"* [John 8:50]. Peter was profoundly and personally aware that Jesus continued this witness all the way to the cross: *"When they hurled their insults at him, he did not retaliate; when he suffered, he made no threats. Instead, he entrusted himself to him who judges justly"* [1 Peter 2:23].

Jesus Christ will be our judge on the last day, but only because the Father has chosen to judge *"men's secrets through Jesus Christ"* [Romans 2:16; Acts 17:31].

Jesus spoke in depth concerning his place as the one who is to judge. As in everything else, however, he points to the Father. The following is particularly instructive:

> *"As for the person who hears my words but does not keep them, I do not judge him. For I did not come to judge the world, but to save it. There is a judge for the one who rejects me and does not accept my words; that very word which I spoke will condemn him at the last day. For I did not speak of my own accord, but the Father who sent me commanded me what to say and how to say it. I know that his command leads to eternal life. So whatever I say is just what the Father has told me to say."*
> [John 12:47-50]

Jesus points to the Father as the ultimate source of all judgement. On the last day the words he spoke will enact judgement. True he spoke those words which will condemn the one who rejects him, but those words weren't his - they were the Father's words. The Father told him what to say and even how to say it! It is the Father's word which will judge: just as it was the Father's word which was spoken by the Son, it is the Father's judgement which is enacted by the Son.

Of course, Jesus is more than the one who *speaks* the word. He *is* the Word made flesh [John 1:1,14]. But the Word has been sent *by* the Father and is the perfect word *about* the Father [John 1:18]. Jesus is not an independent agent. He can do nothing by himself. He has come not to do his own will but the Father's will. When he judges he cares only about judging in accordance with his Father's will [Mark 14:36; John 4:34]: his aim is to please him [John 5:30].

This makes sense: Jesus is the perfect revelation of the Father. Just as Jesus is the revelation of the Father's love, for example, he is also the perfect revelation of the Father's just judgement. In him, as we enter a restored relationship with the Father, we too give witness to the truth about the one who really is the Judge: he is "just". But there's more: he is also "... *the one who justifies those who have faith in Jesus.*" [Romans 3:26]

BOOK ONE:
THE COURTROOM

Part Three

Counterfeit Judges:
What We're Doing Here

†

Chapter 6

JUDGEMENT:
Sowing and Reaping

Judgement: "If you're on the seat, you will receive!"

> *"Do not judge, or you too will be judged. For in the same way you judge others, you will be judged, and with the measure you use, it will be measured to you."* [Matthew 7:1-2]

Only a judge can be judged!

Jesus' teaching concerning the ways of destructive judgement runs counter to what most of us have believed based on our experience. We tend to experience judgement as something we do or something that is done to us; we give it out, we take it in. We don't often see any connection between giving and receiving. In other words, when I *receive* judgement that comes at me from the outside today, I do not associate that with any destructive judging I may have done yesterday, or last month. Jesus shines a corrective light on our experience. He reveals the circuit of judgement which exists in human relationships.

"Do not judge, or you too will be judged". First, Jesus' teaching applies to our relationship with him. I cannot both sit as an idol on the throne of judgement in my own life and be free of the just judgement of the one whose throne I'm sitting on!

"For in the same way you judge others ..." Second, Jesus' words apply to our relationships with one another. He reveals this truth: when I receive judgement from you, I receive it as a judge. Or, to be faithful to the deeper, more scandalous implications of Jesus' teaching, we might put it this way: when I receive judgement from you, I receive it *because* I am a judge!

When I stand as judge over my life, I live with my own judgement of myself, but I also live with your judgement of me, having given you the power to judge me, without intending to. This is easily observed. The more bitterly I accuse you of being a liar, the more sensitive I become to being *called* a liar. So I construct defences to protect myself against any hint that I may not be telling the pure truth! I might try for instance, to undermine the credibility of anyone who seems to be accusing me of lying. Another strategy might involve my projecting the attitude that I couldn't care less what anyone thinks of me. But, regardless of the particulars, if I have defences against perceived judgements of me they are not indications that those judgements have no power. On the contrary, my defences are an acknowledgement of that power.

One might conclude that I defend because my judging somehow makes me *vulnerable* to being judged. But, if we understand Jesus to mean simply and literally what he says, we would have to say that he points to a condition beyond vulnerability. He does not say that if we measure it out, it *may* come back. He says, *"For in the same way you judge others, you will be judged, and with the measure you use, it will be measured to you".* "Will be" is not the same as "may be"!

But is this statement meant to be taken literally? After all, not every true statement is a literal one. When Jesus says *"I am the vine, you are the branches"* [John 15:5] he does not mean to imply that abiding in him will be good for the wine industry. The person who literally cuts off his foot because *"it causes [him] to sin"* [Mark 9:45] is not illustrating fruitful obedience, but rather is exercising a literalism that, because it is misapplied, will simply cripple the sinner while leaving the true root of the sin untouched. But in this passage there is no hint that Jesus' words are to be taken metaphorically. Jesus is revealing a profound application of the law of *"sowing and reaping"* [see Galatians 6:7; 2 Corinthians 9:6], which exposes the ways, means and unavoidable consequences of our judgement. Regardless of whether a law is spiritual, like the law of sowing and reaping, or physical, like the law of gravity, a law is not something to which we are vulnerable. A physical or spiritual law is something to which we are subject. When we judge, measure will follow measure as impact follows a fall.

This is not difficult to understand when it concerns our relationship with God. Apart from the mercy of the Father, found in his Son, our judging will certainly be measured back to us on the day of judgement, simply because, in Adam, our rebellious usurping of God's place as judge of our lives (and all the works of judgement that come from that rebellious root) came under God's judgement. "Matthew 7" judgement remains under judgement. God is not mocked. The days of rebellion are numbered. *"...judgement without mercy will be shown to anyone who has not been merciful"* [James 2:13].

But how about the judgement we visit on other human beings: are there always consequences in this present life? Will my judgement of you return to me exactly as I have dished it out? Sometimes it is difficult to see that exchange operating. On the other hand, there are many times when it is painfully obvious. For instance, I accuse you of being a lazy person. Offended, you lie in wait, looking for evidence of laziness in me. When you find it - and you certainly will find what you're looking for, whether it's there or not - I hear about it, probably with the additional charge of hypocrisy. But often there is no time lapse between the measure going out and the measure coming back:

"You know what the problem with you is? You don't care about anybody but yourself!"

"Oh really!? Well, isn't that lovely; especially coming from the most self-centred person I know!"

On the other hand, this same circuit can be the path of blessing: what if the "measure we use" is mercy? Jesus implies that if my judgements are fully informed by his *mercy*, that mercy too will return to me in like measure. In other words, the whole circuit of mercy will be open in me if I give away what I have received. Though mercy may return to me from the person to whom it was extended, experience says loud and clear that that is not always the case. Nevertheless, Jesus is saying that it will return! How will it return? God will "return" it to me! Or to put it more precisely, I will *continue to receive* the full measure of God's mercy if I do not withhold from others the mercy I have received from him *[again:* James 2:13; *but the perfect illustration is found here:* Matthew 18:23ff*].*

In the same way, my unmerciful, *destructive* judgement may not return to me from the person I have judged. I may find myself receiving judgement at the office from the boss in the same way I have dispensed judgement to you at the breakfast table. But as far as judgement goes, it only takes one person for the whole circuit to be in operation! Very commonly I am both the one who measures it out *and* the one who measures it back. My life is impacted by my judgements even when no other person is directly involved. Here is an "every day" example from a woman who came to have a deep awareness of the ways and means of judgement in her life:

The shallow mum

I had an important speaking engagement scheduled out of state, and my mother called and asked me how I was coming along with my preparations. After letting her know that I was solid on some of my talk but I still had a great deal to work out, she replied, "Don't worry. I know you'll do fine. What are you planning to wear?" After ending the conversation, I felt let down. What I had hoped to hear from her was a desire to discuss my subject matter - to show some interest in what was important to me. But all I got was, "What are you planning to wear?" "How ridiculous!" I thought. "My mother is a shallow woman."

A few months later, my sons, who were both church organists and in their early twenties, had an opportunity to go to Boston to visit twelve historic organs in one day. When they came home, they were full of excitement as they shared their day. On and on they went. Everything started to sound the same and it became tedious to listen to - so much detail that I had no interest in. When I thought I couldn't listen to another story, I asked, "What did you eat?" Immediately my heart condemned me. "I am a shallow woman," I thought. My earlier judgement of my mother had come back to bite me.

The effect of the judgement in this example was relatively mild and short lived. By way of contrast, in the following example we see a judgement which, though it too was never voiced out loud, had a significant and sad effect on the life of a family for years.

No baby-sitter for us

Once, as a young wife and mother, I was at a gathering where I overheard people talking about someone who had taken her mother into her home. They said that the mother had only been taken in so that she could be used as a "built-in babysitter". "How awful and unfair was that!" these women whispered. I never said anything. But, although I did not realize it then, I know now that my heart agreed with and took hold of that judgement.

Eventually I took on the responsibility of having my mother come to live with my husband and me and our children. When mother moved in I was determined never to "use" her that way. "I must never have my mother baby-sit." When a social event would come around and we had need of a baby-sitter, I was worried that if I hired someone else my mother would think we didn't trust her. This went on for years. My husband and I never had time alone. Once in awhile we would dream about going away for a weekend, but the same old fears would smack me. I was determined not to have people talk about me "using" my mother, and by no means was I about to hurt my mother's feelings by hiring someone else. We never left home without the children.

Long after the children had grown, I had great remorse in recognizing how I had deprived my husband. My fear of judgement, which of course is rooted in judgement itself, had kept me and my husband from many joys. This judgement had built prison walls around our lives. The only "pay-off" was a certain kind of self-righteousness—not very gratifying! I realized the wrong I had done to my husband and to our relationship. I saw that I had deprived my mother of some of the joys of being a grandmother and of a more active partnership in the family life. I had also deprived my children. Finally, in the face of all this, I had to deal with self-judgement!

Spitting in the wind

Clearly, the "measure" we receive is not dependent upon the measure we get back *from other people*. *"For in the same way you judge others, you will be judged"* applies when I judge you, but you do not judge me in return, and, as we have seen, it applies even when I am not aware that I have made any judgement at all and/or when I have never expressed it outwardly. Apparently, the law Jesus refers to is like the law we encounter when we spit directly into a strong wind. Again, it is not "vulnerability" that best describes the situation. What if you see that I'm about to spit directly into a wind: how much help is it going to be to me for you to yell, "Don't do it! Your face will be vulnerable?" It would be much kinder if you yelled, "If you spit now you'll wear it!" Better not to foster any illusions, especially when there is a physical or spiritual law involved.

When we judge, we're spitting in the wind. It doesn't matter if the one we're spitting at blows us a kiss in return, we *will* receive the measure we have launched right back in our face! Count on it.

The heart of a judge: a closer look

How, exactly, does this work? How does my judging give others the power to judge me? Why does my act of judgement cause me to receive the same judgement I dispense, even if I never really dispense it, and even if no other person is directly involved? Jesus offers us the key. The heart of the matter is the heart:

"You brood of vipers! How can you speak good things, when you are evil? For out of the abundance of the heart the mouth speaks. The good person brings good things out of a good treasure, and the evil person brings evil things out of an evil treasure."
[Matthew 12: 34f]

"Then he said, 'Are you also still without understanding? Do you not see that whatever goes into the mouth enters the stomach, and goes out into the sewer? But what comes out of the mouth proceeds from the heart, and this is what defiles. For out of the heart come evil intentions, murder, adultery, fornication, theft, false witness, slander. These are what defile a person.'" [Matthew 15:16-20a]

The defiling work of judgement begins right at home in our own heart. It can come as a shock to us when we realize that we *welcome the judgement that can hurt us so much.* But we do. We give power to others to visit judgement on us by constructing a place in our heart where judgement comes knocking and hears a nice warm "Welcome!" We will not - we cannot - receive judgement from others unless we have a place in us where that judgement has a "home". Judgement cannot visit where it is not welcomed and where it has no place to stay.

I repeat: without intending it, we create strongholds in our hearts - strong, welcoming, well protected places - where the judgement of others is received. A "stronghold" is established around the things that our hearts embrace. In order for me to judge you I must first take hold of that judgement, say "yes" to it, make space for it and give it power. This is almost certainly not what I intend. I think that I am going to take hold of judgement for my own temporary purpose: I think (or act as though I think), "I'll take it into my hand and fling it at you and you'll get what you have coming and that's the end of that." But that isn't the end of that: it's only the beginning. When I judge, my rebellion brings me under the power of deception. The truth is that no human being can *use* judgement. Judgement is an idolatrous, occult power and *it uses us.*

Taking judgement into my heart is like taking an enemy into my home. I think he will be useful to me; that he will stay put and remain safely locked up until I let him out to serve me by helping me secure something for myself that I think I need - perhaps by functioning as a weapon I can use in some battle out there in the world. But he doesn't stay put! He roams around seeking something to destroy. He plots against me from the inside, unlocks my doors at night, and is a friend to all who wish me harm. He tempts me to judge, then condemns me for judging. He spreads lies about me and collaborates with all the cursing and deception aimed at me from the world around me. He sows thorns in the soil of my heart. He poisons my cup.

Drinking poison

Destructive judgement seems so right - tastes so good - to our "fallen" flesh! But when we drink it, what are we drinking, really? I have heard it said that when we refuse to forgive we are, in effect, "drinking poison and waiting for the other guy to die"! So it is when we drink from the cup of judgement. It doesn't matter whether or not we have outwardly offered that poison to someone else. If we drink it then *we* ourselves are poisoned. Period. But there is more: judgement is a poison that, because it is like a "universal solvent", cannot be kept in any container. (Think of it: if you invented the "universal solvent", what would you keep it in?) It leaks out and spreads through every part of our being: body, mind and spirit.

So, as we have seen, we don't need to pronounce judgement outwardly; no one else need be directly involved at all. As we judge, so we are judged, because whether or not we give it away, having been embraced, *it remains with us*. When we draw and drink contempt from the poisoned well of our hearts, the well remains full. Though we spit it out, we end up wearing it.

Chapter 7

OUT OF THE GARDEN

Out of the Garden: The Place of Loss

It would be hard to find an exact analogy in everyday life for the loss we suffered in the "fall", especially if we take into account the lethal nature of that loss. After all, if I lose a hoe I can buy another. If I lose the hand that holds the hoe, even then, life goes on. If I used that hand to earn my living, I can find another way to earn my bread. There are other jobs. I can survive, though it might be very difficult: it may mean a big change in the quality of my life or the amount of time I have to work to maintain the quality I have (the earth may yield its increase grudgingly). Regardless, I was not made for the hoe, I don't need my hand to live, and I don't have to be a farmer. What we lost in the garden must have more to do with things that we cannot do without, like air to breathe or essential nourishment for our physical life.

As Christians we know from scripture that what we lost was the "right" relationship we had with God [ex. Romans 5:18ff]. But why is that such devastation? How can a relationship be of such critical importance? Suppose there is a love relationship at the centre of my life; I find myself saying, "I was made for you and you were made for me. You are my life!" But what if you are taken from me?

No matter how important you were to me, regardless of the suffering, life would go on! That is, unless I decide that I don't wish it to continue. But that would be a choice I make, not a necessary consequence of our separation, no matter how adamant I may be that my life is "over". Why? Because the absolute truth is that I was not made for you, nor you for me and we are not the source of life for one another.

Scripture reveals, however, that we were made for a relationship - a relationship that was, literally, life for us. This life did not come about through an accident. We did not come into existence through chance or as a result of the action or outworking of impersonal and purely material forces. We know the truth: we were created, and created purposefully. We were shaped for God by the hands of God. This is an obvious, but nonetheless foundational truth which sheds light on our human "fallen" condition, especially as that concerns the nature of what we lost when we "fell". What did we lose? We lost all we were made to receive from the One for whom we were shaped.

The "shape" we're in

So what were we meant to receive? In what shape were we made? To discover this, it will be useful to begin with a little talk about the birds and the bees. Or, better yet, the birds and the hippos. We can begin with the hummingbird. If you watch them going about their business, you'll see that God made hummingbirds perfectly. They're made just right for the life they lead.

But think of this: what would have happened if God had made the hippopotamus and said to the hippo, "Go forth now and hover over that tiny flower and draw forth its nectar and be satisfied!"? Picture that. This would not result in happiness for the hippo; certainly not for the flower.

But if God said the same thing to the humming bird, and he did, things would turn out just right. Why? Because she was made for the flower and the flower was made for her. They go together perfectly. The humming bird has this long pointed beak that's just right for getting all the way down there into that long neck flower where the nectar is. But that's not all: the humming bird is a hover craft. He can stay right there in one place making whatever tiny little adjustments are needed so the connection is perfect. Not just any bird would do. A seagull has a long beak but imagine what a mess she'd make of a tiny flower! She's too big and she hasn't got the right wings for it.

Like the humming bird (and the hippopotamus, of course), human beings were made for something - for a purpose. We were made for God. Because God *is* life and the source of our life, we were made in the shape of life with him. In other words, we were made in just the right "shape" for a personal relationship with God. So, we do not have the life intended for us in creation apart from the relationship for which we were made.

This is born out in our experience when we are born again by the Spirit. When we come to experience the joy of life with him, we know that we were made for that joy. This joy is, as Peter says, a taste of glory, beyond anything that can be expressed [1 Peter 1:8]. This joy is, in part, the result of the thanksgiving for new life that wells up in our hearts. We are fulfilled in this thanksgiving because we were made in the shape of thanksgiving for the gift of life - and for the giver of the gift!

But there is more. Because God is all=powerful, we were made in the shape of awed reverence and holy fear. Because the one who made us is both our judge and our Lord, we were made in the shape of obedience and for his lordship. The only way we can love him is through obedience. The only freedom we can know is under his lordship.

And we have seen that we were created to be children of a perfectly loving Father. Because God the Father *is* love, we were formed with the capacity (*and the need*) to receive his love and to love him in return.

We were made for one Lord, one Judge, one Father. We were made to live in the freedom of that created relationship. Regardless of the lies we may grip in desperation, nothing else satisfies and there is no other freedom. *Human freedom is the power to be who we were created to be.* We are satisfied in the depths of our souls and spirits only when we live in child-like trust, submitted to the Father's will and to his embrace of love. That is the only "right" relationship there is with God. We are satisfied in it because that is what we were shaped for.

That is the picture of human life with God as he intended it - before deception and rebellion enter in to the world. In the light of this truth we see the depth of our loss. Following their rebellion against God, Adam and Eve were expelled from the Garden of Eden. Obviously they left behind much more than real-estate. Though their rebellion took them out of the garden, it was most essentially a path away from the *maker* of the garden and from the life intended for them there with him. Their rebellion had brought about a deadly relational separation from God. Scripture reveals this condition of estrangement to be nothing less than a gaping, unbridgeable chasm between humanity and the source of its life. It was this deadly distance that Jesus spanned through his obedient life and death.

Out of the Garden: What We Lost

But what, precisely, did we lose through our choice to take God's place - to try to "be like" God - to strike out on our own? The answer to that will have everything in the world to do with the practical daily outworking of our judging ways. But before we explore the direct connection between our loss and our judgement (in the next chapter), we need to understand more specifically what it was that we lost.

Simply put, our loss, as we have seen, can be described this way: since we were made for God, our rejection, "in Adam", of God's rightful place as the source and centre of our lives meant the loss of those things we were created to receive from him and of the life we were meant to live with him.

First, we were made with an identity unique in all creation: we were made in God's image to be God's children, to receive his love and return it. *Second,* we were made to live from God's provision and under his protection. *Third*, we were created in such a way that our lives would have purpose, meaning and fulfilment through the doing of God's will. Our "doing" would come as a consequence of our "being". Namely, we would do what children of the Father do. The Father would give us good, challenging, creative, fulfilling work to do, all of it being the perfect expression of our created human nature. Because we were made in his image, our lives would be an accurate and fruitful reflection of his divine nature. Through our being and our doing we would give him glory. In other words, in and through our lives we would express something of the radiant beauty and truth of who he is. That would be our purpose!

Here is the sum of our loss: in Adam, we lost what we were intended to receive from our relationship with God the Father: *personal identity, provision and purpose.*
We will look now at each of these three losses, in more detail.

Lost: Personal Identity

God formed Adam, breathing life into him [Genesis 2:7]. Do we belong to the One who breathes life into us? Yes, we do. *"Know that the Lord is God. It is he who made us and we are his"* [Psalm 100:3]. The psalmist refers to a kind of belonging that is rooted in the infinite power of the sovereign Lord who created all things. In this sense, Adam and Eve belonged to the God who made them as the pot belongs to the potter [Isaiah 29:16, 64:8; Romans 9:21].

But there is another kind of belonging. Adam and Eve were more than pots belonging to a potter - they were children belonging to a father. This, I believe, is the deepest meaning of our being *"made in his image"* [Genesis 1:26-27]. It is not just that *"... the Lord is God. It is he who made us and we are his."* The psalmist continues, *"We are his people, the sheep of his pasture..."*. Our Father's love is as awesome as his sovereign power (in fact it is the ultimate expression of that power): *"...the Lord is good and his love endures forever..."* [Psalm 100:5]. Adam and Eve belonged to God as children belong to their father and their mother. This was God's will and purpose for them: all that was his was to be theirs; they were to live in the "house" their Father had made for them. There they would belong; they would know him and be known by him; they would receive and give; they would be loved and return that love. Adam and Eve would not only belong to their Father, he would belong to them.

So, what does it mean that, "in Adam", we rejected God as our Father? What does it mean to lose a father? There is no doubt concerning the devastation of that loss in human life. The desolation of the fatherless is obvious and observable everywhere. We can read of it in historical accounts; we can see its effects on the streets of our cities, in the classrooms of our schools, in the pews of our churches. Some of us know and have suffered from that loss in our own lives, even if our father was physically present. But the revelation of scripture is that "in Adam" all humanity is Fatherless.

The loss of our Father means the loss of our identity as his children. This is because it is the Father who tells us who we are. We are whoever the Father says we are! Even in the best of circumstances this is only true of our earthly father in the most limited way. But it is absolutely true with our heavenly Father. We could not possibly exaggerate the importance of this. Let's face it, God is God: who I am to God *is who I am*! If he does not "know" who I am, *I have no "being"* [Matthew 7:23]. On the other hand, his word of love and affirmation and belonging is the Word of my identity, for which I was made.

The Father's words to the only begotten Son become his words to us when we are born from above: *"You are my son, whom I love. With you I am well pleased."* [Mark 1:11] When we hear and receive this word spoken into our hearts by our heavenly Father, it brings us again under the banner of blessing that came in our creation when God pronounced that creation "good". We become a new creation by the power of that indwelling Word of Life. We know, at last, who we were made to be. His word answers our deepest questions.

But in order to become what I was created to be, I must receive something more than knowledge. The loss of my identity was not the result of my forgetting something. That loss, in Adam, results in the fact that I am not, in truth, the Father's child any more. I no longer have the life and blessing of that relationship. And I cannot make myself his child through my own efforts. That relationship was like a pot that I had the power to smash, but which I don't have the power to put back together. I must receive the power to *be* again. And so it is only by God's power that, in the "second Adam", identity as the Father's child is given, in his Son, by the Spirit [Romans 8:15-17; John 3:3-8].

The loss of our identity puts *us* - and everything that is essential about us - in question. Those questions concern our *being;* they concern the *love* and *belonging* that are the bedrock of the life for which we were made. Those questions are a deep ache, an inarticulate longing, a desperate plea: *"Who am I? Am I loved? Am I loveable? To whom do I belong?"* We may be aware, at least to a limited extent, of these questions. In our history there are records of one humanly constructed answer after another. They are houses of cards without the power to make us new. On the other hand we may live our whole lives vaguely aware of that emptiness, but never able to articulate the question.

Regardless of our awareness or lack of it, without the One we were made for - the One for whom our souls and bodies, our minds and spirits were shaped - we remain like a lock never opened; a question never answered. All answers about who we are that are of this fallen world fail to satisfy. What is my identity? "Mother?" What happens when the kids leave or reject me or die? "CEO?" Who am I when I fail, or after they demote me or put me out to pasture? Even more insidious: who am I when I "succeed", or when my family still needs me? Our identity apart from our identity in God is a shifting shadow. That false identity is like a counterfeit rock which quickly disintegrates into wet sand when the wind comes and the rain [Matthew 7:24-27].

Lost: Provision

All our loss comes as a consequence of our rejection of God. First, we lost the one from whom we received our identity. Second, in turning away from God, we turned away from his provision.

God's first provision was, of course, our life! [Genesis 1:27; 2:7] But he also provided the things that nourished and protected that life: good food and drink for our bodies, and the provision of protection from things that would harm us [Genesis 1:29; 2:16-17]. (Remember that the word of prohibition is his loving provision too.)

In providing for us, God our Father does not despise our physical needs, nor does he violate our created reason and will [Genesis 3:21; Joshua 24:15; Isaiah 1:18; 6:8, John 7:16ff]]. He created all these, saw that they were good and blessed them. He provided for us in the context of the abilities he gave us and the *need* we have, in him, *to be who we are*: to be the thinking, willing persons that he made us to be. He didn't provide us with a rocking chair on Eden Porch where we sit daily, waiting to be served - to be, literally, handed everything we need. This plays itself out in many ways:

He created every creature and gives the growth, but we were made to be the agents of his sovereignty on the earth.

We were to tend the garden and gather (or pick!) the harvest.

The Father didn't create "the stork" to deliver much less raise our children.

He told us the truth about good and evil, but he gave us a will and *we needed to obey in order to benefit.*

Jesus addresses the human condition apart from God's provision in this well known passage from the "sermon on the mount":

> *"Therefore I tell you, do not worry about your life, what you will eat or drink; or about your body, what you will wear. Is not life more important than food, and the body more important than clothes? Look at the birds of the air; they do not sow or reap or store*

away in barns, and yet your heavenly Father feeds them. Are you not much more valuable than they? Who of you by worrying can add a single hour to his life? "And why do you worry about clothes? See how the lilies of the field grow. They do not labour or spin. Yet I tell you that not even Solomon in all his splendour was dressed like one of these. If that is how God clothes the grass of the field, which is here today and tomorrow is thrown into the fire, will he not much more clothe you, O you of little faith? So do not worry, saying, 'What shall we eat?' or 'What shall we drink?' or 'What shall we wear?' For the pagans run after all these things, and your heavenly Father knows that you need them. But seek first his kingdom and his righteousness, and all these things will be given to you as well." [Matthew 6:25-33].

We no longer know our provider. We feel we must provide for ourselves and are filled with anxiety. We cry out, "What shall we eat ...what shall we drink...what shall we wear?" Jesus assures us that our heavenly Father knows we need these things and desires to provide them! [see also 7:11]. But, when we do not know our provider, no assurance helps. We may hear that God clothes the flowers - that he even clothes the disobedient [Genesis 3:21], that *"he causes his sun to rise on the evil and the good, and that he sends rain on the righteous and the unrighteous"* [Matthew 5:45b], but we are unmoved. Neither the beautiful clothing of the flowers nor the evident abundance of bird food is a comfort. After all, birds starve, sometimes there's too much sun and the rain doesn't always come when we need it.

Jesus teaches that the problem for us is not located in the provision itself - not in the "having" or the "not having". We can be as enslaved to material things when we don't have them as when we do. We may suppose that real life will begin only when we've acquired enough. Our minds and hearts can be focused on (and captive to) all the stuff we don't have rather than on the provision that is there all around us!

On the other hand, we can be just as anxious about material things when we have them as when we don't. Suppose we have enough? Well, the truth is that it wouldn't matter if we had lakes of water in storage, or many barns filled with grain, our hearts would still be fearful. "We've got all this grain stored up, now we have to guard the barns. The rivers and lakes may dry up. The cisterns may leak or be poisoned." Enough is never enough. John D. Rockefeller was asked, in the face of his great wealth, how much money he thought he needed. "Just a little more" he said. The bottom line is that it doesn't matter whether we have nothing, or everything we could ever "need" - the anxiety (and the bondage) remains.

And what about the provision of God's "protection"? Without that provision, we put our trust in coercive, human power and control - we trust in "horses and chariots" [Psalm 20:7]. But even if we were to have plenty of "horses", no end of "chariots" and we ourselves were as strong as an ox, it wouldn't help. Why? Is it because we are aware of the limitations of all the things we rely upon to keep us "safe" today - that they are subject to an unknown, threatening and uncontrollable tomorrow? Yes, in part. But Jesus teaches that ultimately our anxiety about safety is not founded upon the presence or absence of any specific provision *or threat to it*. There is a deeper foundation.

Jesus' teaching in this passage from Matthew exposes the foundation of our anxiety. As always, he points to the Father: *"Is not life more important than food, and the body more important than clothes ...? But seek first his kingdom and his righteousness, and all these things will be given to you as well"*. This "kingdom", Jesus refers to, is the place where we know God the Father as our provider. Jesus directs our hearts to the Father. Jesus is saying that our anxiety will remain if we set our hearts on provision.

It is true that we may not have the provision and protection for our physical lives that God intended if we are not living in a relationship of loving obedience with our true provider: how can I bring you to the place of provision if you do not listen to me or go where I tell you to go? How can I give you something you need for your life if your heart insists upon having what the world says you need for your pleasure? The deeper truth is that, apart from the provider, provisions become an idol standing in his place [see also Luke 12:15-21]. The root of the problem of lost provision is not provision! The root of our problem is idolatry. When we put provision first, we turn even God's provision into an idol to which we give our hearts. (Witness the so called "prosperity gospel"—a man made "gospel" using Christian vocabulary and tortured, isolated scriptures, all in the service of an acquisitive, greedy idol, who mocks at the foot of the cross.)

Remember the humming bird? The truth is that we were not really made for the flower, but for the maker of the flower. The truth is that we were not made for provisions - we were not made to love provisions. We are made in the shape of thanksgiving for the provisions and for the love they express. Unless we put the provider before (even his!) provision, we live as idolaters who, rather than loving God and using provision, love provisions and attempt to use God to get them.

So, essentially, what we lost as a consequence of the fall was this "kingdom" to which Jesus refers: the place where God the Father gives the life and gives the growth; where we gather and give thanks; where we hear and obey in trust; where he gives to us of his power and authority so that we can do a work that serves his will. Having lost first things, lesser things will not do. Even as we flaunt our "things", overfill our bodies and wave our weapons, we are lost and empty and filled with fear, not because we don't have food, clothing and protection (though we may not), but because we don't have *him*. When we've got him we are absolutely safe, even on a cross, and we have the power to thank him for his provision whether we are, in the words of the Apostle Paul, "well fed or hungry, whether living in plenty or in want [Philippians 4:12]." *The Father* is provision for his children.

Just as was the case with lost personal identity, the loss of our provider *and* his provision, brings questions that preoccupy our hearts day by day: *"What shall I eat? What shall I drink? What shall I wear?"* But nothing brings more profound anxiety than the question that rises from the loss of the provision of God's protection: *"Am I safe?"* Our perceived need to answer that question positively by trying to secure (preserve) our own lives on every level, creates a landscape that is littered with millions of individual men and women - with whole nations - enslaved to greed and avarice, held in the grip of addiction and mangled by the machines of war.

Lost: Purpose

> *"Then God said, 'Let us make man in our image, in our likeness, and let them rule over the fish of the sea and the birds of the air, over the livestock, over all the earth, and over all the creatures that move along the ground.' So God created man in his own image, in the image of God he created him; male and female he created them. God blessed them and said to them,*

101

'Be fruitful and increase in number; fill the earth and subdue it. Rule over the fish of the sea and the birds of the air and over every living creature that moves on the ground.' ' [Genesis 1:26-28]

"The LORD God took the man and put him in the Garden of Eden to work it and take care of it." [Genesis 2:15]

"Now the LORD God had formed out of the ground all the beasts of the field and all the birds of the air. He brought them to the man to see what he would name them; and whatever the man called each living creature, that was its name. So the man gave names to all the livestock, the birds of the air and all the beasts of the field." [Genesis 2:19-20]

Here we have descriptions of God's will for human "doing". It was in the doing of his will as they lived out their true identity as his children that Adam and Eve were to know purpose in their lives. The work that God assigned to them was not some kind of servile drudgery. It was good, creative, challenging work - a "doing" that would be both fulfilling and, especially, fruitful! God spoke of that fruitfulness directly in his call to "increase in number", but fruitful multiplication was also to come as the ground of the garden was worked, and God's living, growing things were tended, bore fruit and increased, thirty, sixty - even one hundred fold [Matthew 13:8]! Since Adam and Eve were made in God's image, the fruitful outcome from their labours - whether through begetting or tending - was meant to be, in effect, a word about the true nature of the One who *is* fruitfulness and the God of multiplication, "spoken" in their fleshly life.

God's infinite creative, sustaining love would also be reflected in the one-flesh union of husband and wife; there in Eve's body, heart, mind and spirit, as she carried, birthed, nurtured and raised up new life; there in Adam as he entered into the work he was given to do, naming the creatures as the first step in the exercise of the authority and dominion given to him. There as they were together as partners in a God-centred relationship of love, using their creative, God-given gifts of mind, body and spirit, glorifying God and experiencing the fulfilment of their created nature.

It would seem, perhaps, that things haven't changed. We can (and do!) have a sense of meaning, purpose and fulfilment in many of the common things of life that offer opportunities for the expression of our God given abilities: drawing a picture, solving a mechanical problem, baking a cake, piloting a plane, guiding our little girl through a grouchy afternoon, climbing a mountain, crafting a cabinet, growing a rose.

One might ask, "In what sense, then, has human purpose been lost? After all, human beings still *seem* to find purpose in life through what they do." And, although it is certainly the case that some of those who experience their lives as having purpose are persons of faith who are seeking to know and do God's will, one does not have to be a Christian to have a sense of purpose. Possible examples are beyond number; some common and some extraordinary. Countless lives have been dedicated, for example, to the pursuit of "causes": the spread of revolutionary ideologies, the advancement of knowledge in a variety of scientific fields, the tireless effort to "educate the masses" about various kinds of perceived danger to the public welfare, or, perhaps, about the human benefits that come from exposure to and involvement in the arts, religion, recreation, etc. The pursuit of a cause or a passion for or against something can become the avowed meaning and purpose of any human life, and experienced as such by the person.

So the question remains: why, and in what sense, did the loss of a "right" relationship with God result in the loss of purpose in human life? The answer is that it didn't! Nor did it result in the loss of identity or provision. It resulted in the loss of the identity, provision and purpose *intended for humanity by God*, and which only comes in the context of a right relationship with him.

That loss is critical, because God's gifts of identity, provision and purpose are not just one set of options for humanity. His will for us in these terms is in perfect harmony with our created nature! As we have seen, we are formed for God. Unless we live for and from the one who formed us, we become *de*formed. That is precisely the human condition: *souls, minds, hearts and spirits shaped by and for God, now warped and twisted by conformity to the shape of idols: alien identities, provisions and purposes.*

So, we can live with a sense of purpose which is not our created purpose, just as we can live with an identity that is not our created identity. We can derive a sense of meaning and purpose in the expression of natural, creative gifts of mind and body, even when they are not the outworking of loving obedience and service to God. This should not surprise us: it is not different from the fact that human beings can experience purely physical pleasure in the sexual act outside of the divinely intended context and purposes for that act. But our subjective experience is not the truth. The truth is that the false-self lives a false life: all human efforts and "purposes" that proceed from humanly fabricated identities are in the service of sin [Romans 14:23].

Many people live with a sense of some purpose but never know the *true* purpose of their lives. For them the questions, *"Why am I here? What is the meaning and purpose of my life?"* may seem to have an answer, but that answer does not reflect the truth of their created purpose. But isn't it better to have *some* purpose, even if it isn't God's purpose? The answer is simply, "NO!" If I have a false sense of purpose I am in a *worse* position than if I had no sense of purpose at all! After all, is my situation any less desperate because, though I am blind, I think I can see? No. It is *more* desperate! [John 9:41]

But what about those who live with no abiding sense of purpose? For them, even if their lives are filled with what appears to be productive work, even if they seem to achieve significant things, anxiety and a nagging sense of futility persists. None of what they do satisfies for long and at the end of the day the questions remain: *"Do my accomplishments mean anything? Is there any worth, or real, lasting purpose to my life?"* How often have the popular icons of our age answered that question for themselves with a fatal overdose of the same things which medicated them through the terrors of an applause-filled past?

Loss: the last two don't count!

Let us be explicit: the loss of our created identity *is the root cause* of the other kinds of loss in human life. Earlier we said that, though there are three scriptural reasons for not judging, "the first two don't count"! We could say something similar about what we lost in the fall: we lost three things, but the last two don't count! All human loss stems from the foundational loss of our identity. The fulfilment of God's saving plan reflects this truth by addressing that fundamental loss: when God's saving power meets us in the Holy Spirit, we are met by, and literally given, the power and the right to become a child of the Father again [John 1:12]. "The Father's child" becomes our identity, as God intended it in creation. Paul puts it this

105

way: by the power of the Holy Spirit we have a new identity: "son" [Romans 8:15f]! "Son", because we have that new identity only in God's Son, whose righteous relationship with the Father is given to us by the Holy Spirit. What a gift! This meets us in our deepest need, because *we cannot have what we were intended to have, or do what we were intended to do, unless we become the person we were intended to be.* So, the great news is that the restoration of our true identity results in the restoration of God's intended provision and purpose.

The key to all of this, especially as it concerns our purpose, is that, in Jesus Christ, we begin to do the things that "sons" do! That is key because our "doing" was meant to come from our "being". But when we lost our identity as children of God, we became lost wonderers, all our actions *driven* by a thirst to know who we were, so that we could *be* again! "Driven", because human beings can't live without an identity. Every human person has been made in the shape of a God-given identity.

Having lost that, every human being is in the business of trying to fabricate an identity on his or her own. In that desperate and doomed effort, the purpose of all that humans do becomes twisted:

Instead of being an outward expression (one might say a consequence) of our identity (our being), our "doing" becomes a means for defining, establishing and maintaining that identity.

We chose, through our doing, *not to be* who we were created to be. In Adam we chose to become someone by doing something. Now we live under that judgement: we have to *do something* so that we can *be someone*. The answer to the question, "Who am I?" becomes, "I am what I do!" As God's creatures, made in his image, we began with, "I am, therefore I think!" But human philosophies reflect, accurately, the fallen human state: "I think, therefore I am" [Descartes]. This is creation turned on its ear. And for us in day to day life, it is a pathetic enterprise. Witness:

"I did something bad" leads to, "I *am* bad."

"If I can force myself to do enough good, maybe I'll *become* good enough to deserve love and *be* (acceptable)." (Christians can be particularly susceptible to this one!)

If I believe that you have failed to meet my expectations - that you have failed to meet my need - that failure in the arena of *doing* results in a judgement about your *being*:

"You *are* a failure!"

"You didn't understand me: you *are* stupid!"

Of course the same thing goes on in our relationship with ourselves:

"I didn't win: I *am* a loser!"

And so it goes. These are lines from a courtroom tragedy: the script of human loss and our desperate efforts to secure for ourselves what God intended to give in the relationship for which we were created.

We turn now to look more closely at life in the courtroom. What is the relationship between destructive judgement and all the human loss suffered through rebellion and deception? There on the judgement seat do we act as judges in a random way and just for the lack of anything else to do? Or, is there a purposeful pattern to it ... a hidden courtroom agenda? What is our courtroom life all about, really?

✝

Chapter 8

Into the Courtroom:
The Function of Judgement in the Place of loss

The Agenda of Loss

Hell on earth

One excellent definition of sin is this: "Sin is the human attempt to take by force what God would give by grace." Apart from the saving, transforming work of God, accomplished in us, we are all in the business of attempting to secure for ourselves what God freely gave us in creation, but which we lost "in Adam". In that light we can see the fruit of our futile attempts to secure these things for ourselves - to create and maintain an identity, provide for our many needs and find meaning and purpose in our lives: those attempts simply contribute to the ongoing sickness and destruction of our relationships with God, ourselves and one another.

The seductive idea of being "like God" sounded like heaven to us. But the reality of actually having to *be* god for ourselves is hell on earth. As little lost gods, the biggest impediment we have to overcome is that we are not, in point of fact, God. We're not "all wise"; not "all powerful". This is a huge problem: how are we going to get what we need if we can't understand and manage everything? But we seldom look at the truth of our powerlessness. Instead we adopt any number of strategies in our desperate attempt to stay "in the driver's seat". But it's a sham - almost comic. We're like a little child "steering" a tiny plastic car our daddy pushes around the yard for us: our little hands grip and attempt to steer with something that isn't connected to the wheels! The most convincing proof of our condition is this: if and when we do eventually "give up control" to the God who *is* God, we find that we haven't lost it! Instead we become aware of the truth that all we have lost is the *illusion* of control. We accept the truth that we never had much in the first place.

Counterfeit life, grounded in deception, is never a very pretty picture. Nevertheless, we are going to take a brief but closer look at that picture before we move on to see how all this relates to judgement.

Here is the picture: when we are driven by the attempt to "manage" everything we live in destructive futility. Just when we think we have things tied down, the world gets turned on its ear - sometimes overnight. Everything from storms to stock markets are liable to come crashing down in our so carefully constructed world. Or, as we have seen, having "secured" the things we think we need, we live in fear of losing them - they begin to "have" us! And we are not alone in this scramble. Others are up to the same thing we're up to. Sometimes we want what we think others have - approval, the latest "stuff", "security" - and we covet. Or it may be the other way around: we may look at one another with disdain from what we believe is a superior position. We might call this counterfeit life, "life-by-comparison". But regardless of whether we stand on the soil of covetousness or of disdain, it is all the same soil: it is all sandy soil, shifting under our feet, being subject to the erosion that comes with rain and to the destructive, uprooting effect of every worldly wind that blows [Matthew 7:24-27].

When I "have it made" I don't have it made - I might say *especially* then. Even if I've "arrived" and the world is at my feet, my expensively procured fans get bored, stop applauding me, and start throwing things. No mystery here: "they" get to feel like they have control in their own lives by hoisting me up then tossing me down. I understand. I'm in the same business - we're all in the same business out there in the world and right at home. We're in the business of trying to use people to get what we think we need.

In order for you to be useful to me I must try to control you. Manipulation is the name of the game. My repertoire is extensive: it might include shaming, "sweet-talking", doing "good deeds" in order to "buy" the approval/acceptance of others, intimidation, flattery, or "guilt-tripping". One primary purpose is to try to get you to change. Of course I'm not acting for your sake (even when I think that's what I'm doing) but because I need you to change so that you will stop doing what you're doing and do other things for my sake.

And what if I "succeed"? What if I find a way to exert the necessary power over you to keep you locked up to serve me? I find that I can't put you in the prison of my need without being there myself. I can't stand with my boot on your neck, pressing you into the muck, without being in the muck myself. Standing there on you I may think that I can see greener pastures over the wall, but I'm still in prison. I may be a bit more physically comfortable, but neither of us is going anywhere.

(Actually, as I stand on you, *you may* be on the road to freedom there, even with no change in your circumstance. If Jesus comes near; presses his face down into the muck with you - if you look into his eyes and see the clean, pure well of his love for you - you may begin to experience free and abundant life right there under my boot. But I won't: I can't!)

111

Without God becoming God for us, this is an endless round, without hope. But there is a way out. If God *can* be God for us, then we don't need to try to be God anymore; we can just be who we are. What a relief! So, what if we hear the "Good News" about a way out of our desperate situation? Faced with heaven, is it possible that any might choose to continue on in hell? Encountered by the Gospel of the one who has come as the answer to all our true needs - especially the need to be loved, accepted and secure - are there any who would continue in the futile attempt to secure everything for themselves? Having heard of the One who has genuine life to give, would anyone continue to try to manufacture his or her own false life? Yes. Jesus makes this clear: *even for those in whose "soil" the seed of the word of God's kingdom is growing*, the deceived, fear-driven pursuit of the world's counterfeit life can persist like deadly thorns which choke out the kingdom seed. Such people go on their way, even in the Church, but it is not the way that leads to fruitful life in the kingdom of God:

"Now the parable is this: The seed is the word of God. The ones on the path are those who have heard; then the devil comes and takes away the word from their hearts, so that they may not believe and be saved. The ones on the rock are those who, when they hear the word, receive it with joy. But these have no root; they believe only for a while and in a time of testing fall away. As for what fell among the thorns, these are the ones who hear; but as they go on their way, they are choked by the cares and riches and pleasures of life, and their fruit does not mature." [Luke 8:11-14]

Hell under cover

The old "agenda of loss" can persist, even under the surface of religious life and belief. How might this look? Let us suppose that

I have heard the truth and I respond. After a while I am able to say, sincerely, "I am a Christian; I have new life now; my life is in Jesus." But what if this God I've heard of and begun to respond to, has simply become part of *my life*; a real part of my life, an important part, but ... well, what if it's still *my* life and I'm still in the business of trying to "secure for myself what God would give me by grace?" In that case, God is now another *resource* I use in my pursuit of an old agenda. I try to use the resource called "God" to get the things I think I need. I hear that trust is the thing. It's all about faith. So I put my trust in the God I need. I have confidence in him: he will enrich, improve, enhance and, in general, fix up *my* life; the life which, I tell myself, is now "found in him".

Before I knew about God, I kept running into immovable objects. I was continually surprised and wounded by things I didn't see coming. But now I begin to trust that if I say, believe and do the right things, life will smooth out and I will know less pain, fear and defeat. The word about God's sovereignty has been sown in my heart. He is all-powerful. He's in control. Finally someone is. It remains for me to figure out *how I must be* and *what I must do* so that he will use his power for my benefit.

The agenda just described reflects the orientation of the old, counterfeit life. This old orientation twists even things intended for blessing - for nourishment in the new life - into things which simply further that false life.

Tithing, for instance: what is tithing for me in the life that is still *my* life? I tithe so that I can prosper. This is exactly what I need - exactly what I've been trying to get without him. But I'm not alone in this enterprise anymore! When I read about tithing or hear teaching about it, what I understand through my filter is this: as a reward for believing in him - part of the salvation package - God wants to give me what I need. More than that, he agrees with me that what I need is more money. So I tithe because that will cause me to prosper. It seems to work for some people; certainly for those who earn their living teaching about it. But, as for me and my household: lose my job. I fall away from church. I take my orientation with me...

Eventually I go to another church where they have a fund for folks out of work. They pay for some job training and, well, things start looking up! I'm solid again. I get involved and make friends. After a few years, one of those friends - a godly man, a husband and father and a leader in the church - has a paralyzing stroke. I know Jesus wants to heal him. I know he can heal him (I've seen it) and I know that he will - it is unthinkable that he will not. I trust. I pray. Many others pray for a long time. But my friend, who has said and believed and done the right things, is not healed. They said that God is "in control". Obviously he isn't. Or, more disturbing, he is and he wanted my friend paralyzed for some purpose. Though it never becomes a conscious thought, deep down in a hidden place within my heart I live in fear that God might want the same for me. Who knows? Gradually I fade from sight and eventually I leave the church altogether.

The previous description was not a parody. It is neither fiction, nor is it uncommon in some form. But it would not have been necessary for the person in this example to leave the church. It is possible to "fall away" and continue to go to church where I live a fruitless life that looks authentic, even abundant, on the outside. It is possible that there is a qualitative difference between the outside of the "cup" and the inside [Matthew 23:25-28]. It is possible that *a huge gap may widen between what I say I believe and what I actually believe as demonstrated by what I live.*

When I live with this "gap" at the centre of my life, I may continue on in the religious enterprise, but I fend for myself in the "real world". Why? Because in the life that remains "my life" - the one I create and maintain and where I'm trying to secure for myself what God would give me by grace - in that life, I have found that God is *utterly unreliable*. He cannot be relied upon to further my agenda. God cannot be trusted to be useful. Why? Because God insists upon being who he is: not a resource in my life, but the *source* of my life. He offers me *his* life, not an enhanced version of my own. I must lose "my life" - the one I'm trying to preserve - if I am to have his [Mark 8:35]. God can only be my provider if he is, first and last and in between, my provision. So the praises that come from my lips on Sunday can come in the midst of the same old desperate, counterfeit life - "life" in a courtroom full of people all trying to do the same thing I'm doing.

The Agenda of Judgement

Roots: Genesis again

We have looked closely at the "loss" we suffered in the Garden and have taken a closer look at some relational patterns imposed upon our lives by the desperate agenda of that loss. Now we need to consider this question: what does our "agenda of loss" have to do with our idolatrous judgement? The answer to that will bring light to a foundational question about life in the "courtroom": What am I really doing as I "sit on the throne" as judge of my life? In other words, "Does my judgement have focus, motive or purpose?" The answer is found in the relationship - and, yes, there is one - between the ways and means of destructive judgement (life in the courtroom) and the things lost in the "fall".

It should come as no surprise that there is a connection between judgement and loss. After all, as we saw when we looked at the "Genesis of Judgement", one was the consequence of the other. The *power behind that connection* was spelled out in Chapter Six.

Based on that understanding we see that when we judged God's word, we took the power of judgement into our hearts intending to use that power to secure some things for ourselves: identity (to be "like God"), vision (to have our "eyes opened") and knowledge (to "know good and evil") [Genesis 3:5]. But, as with all judgement, it was not something that we could use. Rooted as it was in the demonic power of idolatry, judgement used us. Its fruit was death: the loss of all we were intended to receive in the life-giving relationship for which we were made.

Our agenda as judges follows as reaping follows sowing:

As counterfeit judges we try to use the power of judgement to secure for ourselves all that we lost through the power of judgement.

The function of judgement in the place of Loss

The "courtroom" is the "place of loss". If we want to see *how* judgement functions with regard to our "loss" - how our judgement serves the agenda of our loss - that's where we have to look. This sentence from Chapter 1 bears repeating: "This revelation [of the Courtroom] came, I believe, as a gift of sight: the courtroom was a way of seeing a basic orientation of the human heart. It was a way of seeing clearly all the ways of judgement from the most common and apparently trivial to the most dramatic and obviously devastating extremes ..."

Sometimes our eyes are opened to see more clearly, not because our question has been answered, but because a new question has come. This was the case for me concerning the function of judgement with regard to our "loss". It started with a comment from a man who was part of a group studying the "Courtroom" teaching. He began with something like this: "When I look at my own

116

courtroom life as a judge, I have to say that I don't see myself making all that many specific judgements. So it seems like a stretch to say that I'm always on the judgement seat." Then he had a question: "How does this square with the idea that judgement is so fundamentally important and pervasive in my life? In other words, how can it be true that my life is actually being lived out in a courtroom where I sit as judge over my own life *all the time*, if I'm not actually making judgements all the time?"

The question was out in the air. And what a gift it turned out to be. We had to look together at something many of us would say is true in our own lives. First we had to acknowledge that the perception this man had could have been the result of his having found a measure of freedom: perhaps Jesus was on the throne of his heart at times. He would be free for a while, but certain things in his life would cause him to rise up and take the seat back! On the throne, off the throne. He was - we all are - a work in progress.

Second we had to admit that if any of us says that we don't make many specific judgements it may not be the truth; we are, after all, talking about a "hidden enemy." All of us have had to learn to see the judgement in our lives. Jesus is shining light into our darkness, but we don't necessarily see perfectly ... at least not yet. Again, we're a work in progress.

"But hold on!", a woman in the group piped up, "I could say the same thing - I don't seem to make all that many judgements, but I know that my life is full, and I mean absolutely full, of judgement itself! I know I live in the courtroom." "How do you know?" someone asked. "I just know! Jesus is showing me. And what about someone who doesn't know Jesus? Without him on the throne, it's judgement all the time! And I'll bet that many of them would say the same thing: they're not constantly judging everything. And maybe they're right. Even considering that I don't see my own judgement perfectly, I'd still have to say that I don't make judgements constantly. How do I square that with the fact that I know I'm living in the courtroom almost all the time!?"

Good questions. The answers could only come by taking hold of the gift of sight given to us. After all, with the vision of the courtroom had come an invitation: "look at what goes on in a courtroom; see who is there and what they do". So, what do we see if we look more closely?

The Courtroom: A last look.

Significantly, the invitation to look at the courtroom was not just an invitation to look at the judge: "look at what goes on *in a courtroom* ..." Through this wider lens we see that "judgements" constitute only one aspect of life in the courtroom. In fact, only a tiny portion of actual courtroom time is spent in the rendering of a legal judgement concerning guilt or innocence. The vast majority of courtroom time is spent in the presentation, gathering and consideration of *evidence* concerning the case at hand. Even when "judgements" are delivered from the bench during a trial they are largely rulings about the admissibility or inadmissibility *of evidence*.

We see what in retrospect seems obvious: evidence is the life blood of the courtroom. *Everything received there is received as evidence.* The plaintiff, whether it is the "state" or a private individual, prosecutes or brings suit based upon evidence. No matter the particulars - regardless of whether the case is civil or criminal or the court low or high - it's all about evidence. Certainly a defendant gets the picture from the very start when he or she is informed, if taken into custody, that anything they say may be used against them at court. There is no "Time out! This is off the record!" once you become subject to the legal system.

So it is in the spiritual courtroom of this world and of each of our hearts. As judges we are continually gathering evidence. *In so far as we remain the judge of our own lives*, everything that happens to us - all that people say and don't say; the looks we receive; the words of cursing *and of blessing* that come to us - all of it comes as evidence in the core of our being - in the place where the deep agonizing questions live: "Who am I? Am I loved? Am I lovable? Do I belong? Am I safe? Does my life have meaning? Do I have a purpose?"

We gather evidence of our innocence in the face of condemnation. We may even gather evidence to establish our guilt when we have been pronounced innocent! We gather evidence when we are hurt or offended, but also when we are applauded! We gather evidence whether we fail or succeed; whether we find something or lose something; when the pastor speaks to us; when he looks past us; when our friends call; when they don't. We gather evidence to justify the judgement we've already "handed down" and the one for which we've just begun to build a case.

Everything in our life is received as evidence about whether we are loved or unlovable; included or excluded; secure or vulnerable; useful or useless. This is life in the courtroom. It's all about evidence all day every day for the heart where Jesus is *not* enthroned as the only righteous judge.

No wonder that when the call to walk the "more excellent way" of love comes to us in our courtroom [1Corinthians 12:31], it comes as an offensive violation of the legal system in place there! How (our flesh cries out) can we function here - how can we manage our life in this world - if we "keep no record of wrongs" [1Corinthians 13:5]? What? We just throw out all the evidence?! In the New American Bible, the phrase is translated this way: "[love] does not brood over injury". A telling translation. As we accumulate

119

evidence we are often like a hen "brooding" over her eggs. We hatch a "case"; we sit on it; we keep it warm; it grows. And the offspring of that brooding becomes an ugly duckling of our own birthing.

This throws light on a very common pattern of human behaviour: so often we react to others, and they to us, in ways that seem out of proportion to the situation at hand. Why does that one little critical thing I say to you in this moment set off such a strong reaction? Why do these few words from you make me feel far worse – more worthless, rejected and angry - than they "ought" to? Even I may feel shocked by the extreme nature of my own response, and may find myself saying, "Why do I behave this way?" or "Where did *that* come from?"

In the face of this type of experience we may tell ourselves that we have reacted this way because this one relatively minor thing someone said is, after all, the "last straw"! But what *is* the "last straw"? Is it not simply the latest piece of evidence in a long chain of evidence we have been gathering?

When we say "the last straw", we are describing a reaction to something more than the thing that has just happened - more than the "straw" of this moment. We are saying that straws have been gathered over a period of time and bound together in our hearts into one thick bundle that has become too strong for us to break. We no longer have the freedom to respond simply to each little "straw" as it comes to us. Every little straw has been given the power to hit us like a baseball bat, bound up, as it is, to all the others! That one straw might have come as a slap in the face - a slight irritation in the moment - but when we're hit by a two foot thick bundle of straw it has the potential of altering the course of our day! And it often does.

This is true of all of us in so far as we live in the courtroom. The event of this moment is heavier than it appears to be: it carries all the weight of yesterday's events and those of the day before, and so on, way back in some "cases" into the distant past - perhaps so distant that its root is long forgotten.

But we do know the place where the practice of gathering evidence is ultimately rooted. Before we go on to look more deeply at the implications of all this, let's look backward briefly.

The garden: a last look

Just as Genesis [3:1-6] describes human judgement, so too it chronicles the gathering of evidence - that "gathering" and the judging which follows being inseparable. The serpent tempts Eve to enter into the courtroom by tempting her to gather and consider evidence. His method is simple and effective. He tempts and teaches her by setting the example. As the prosecuting barrister, he simply treats God's word as though it is evidence. He puts Eve on the witness stand: "Did God really say...?" Then, taking the stand as a witness for the prosecution, he presents evidence in rebuttal (unsubstantiated, false evidence we might add): "You will not surely die ..." He builds his case for disobedience: "... your eyes will be opened ... you will be like God ... you will know ..."!

Everything that is said and all that is not said comes as evidence in the serpent's courtroom, where Eve has been invited to weigh that evidence and to judge God's word, after due deliberation. Her judgement is based upon the evidence presented. We hear this clearly in the evidentiary justification of the judgement being rendered [vs.6]. From that list it is clear that Eve's judgement of God's word is based upon both the evidence presented to her (she would gain wisdom) and that which she herself has gathered (the apple was "good for food" and "pleasing to the eye"). The gathering of evidence leads to the human embrace of idolatry through the judgement of good and evil.

Chapter 9

In the Courtroom:
It's all about evidence

Love as evidence

The scales of justice

Though it was quite a few years ago, I remember greeting
people after a particular Sunday worship service at the church where
I was serving as pastor and priest. As I stood at the entrance to the
church, Karen (not her real name) came by and we shared a special
hug there in the sunshine. I had been with her in a time of significant
healing the day before. During that prayer time the Father's love and
mercy had touched her in a deep place of rejection and self-loathing.
At several points during the worship service I had seen signs that
looked like fruit from the day before. There seemed to be a depth of
joy and release during times of praise. When I spoke about the
Father's love during the sermon, her face lit up; then tears came - the
kind that are the overflow of a grateful heart - a heart deeply touched
by a love so special that it is known beyond words as the home for
which the heart was made. So this hug of shared celebration.

As I continued to greet others, I saw Karen lingering at the
entrance of the church. She was laughing and enjoying fellowship
with her friends. When I had finished greeting she was still going

strong, obviously unaware that her husband was waiting for her at their car, parked a little way down the street. I had heard him call her name twice - the second time louder than the first. Now I saw him stride up the sidewalk to her, obviously irritated. He interrupted her mid-sentence:

"Don't you remember I said I needed to go straight home after church? I have work to do!"

Karen, clearly upset, said a quick goodbye to her friends and headed off to the car. As they pulled away I saw the pantomime of a heated argument going on in the front seat. As they rounded the corner the last thing I saw was Karen burying her face in her hands.

The next time I met with her (about 2 weeks later) we were back to square one. It was as though every bit of the love she had experienced had leaked out of her.

For most people this picture would be a familiar one. But what is really going on here? It took several years for clarity to come ... with the revelation of the courtroom. Then it was as if a veil had been removed. The revelation was a new way of seeing quickly and simply right to the root of things. Karen was functioning as the judge of her own life. She lived in a courtroom where *everything she experienced was received and weighed as evidence* - most essentially, evidence concerning her identity - concerning the deepest question of her heart: "Am I loved?"

When she experienced the Father's love for her, she received that love *as evidence* that she was loved: powerful evidence; profoundly moving evidence; weighty evidence; but evidence nonetheless. This is the key. In the courtroom evidence is placed on the "scales". The Father's love touched Karen's heart, but she did not fully receive or release it there - she weighed it on scales in her courtroom. Being weighty it pressed those scales down on the "loved" side and Karen became convinced for a while ... until new convicting evidence came, tipping the scales to the other side.

She experienced her life in a way that resembles what we experience when we watch a courtroom drama. The evidence, presented piece by piece by the defendant seems so clear and convincing that we believe it to be the truth. We see no loopholes. Then the prosecutor begins to ask questions. Things begin to get fuzzy. He puts other witnesses on the stand and we hear some complicating, contradicting evidence not presented by the defendant. He throws such a different light on the whole case that our old assurance is torn from us: what had seemed so patently true seems hollow now and unconvincing. Often this happens more than once. We're manipulated one way then the other...

"He's guilty!"

"No, I see now that he's innocent!"

"No, I was right the first time - he's guilty after all!"

"Innocent!"

"Guilty!"

... until time runs out and the script writer is forced to stop dragging us around by the nose.

And so it went day by day for Karen. God The Father had spoken deep into her heart: "You are precious to me!" She had believed this evidence of his love and in the sweet time of her experience she was convinced. Then her husband had presented evidence to the contrary and in a few moments everything had changed for her. The weight of his evidence, *coming into the place where it had a home in her*, had tipped the scales in the other direction...

"Guilty after all! Unworthy! Unloved! Unlovable!"

The "love issue" never settled; the case never closed!

So courtroom life looks a lot like we do when we start picking petals off a daisy: "He loves me. He loves me not." It doesn't matter how many daisies we destroy in our attempt to assure ourselves that "He loves me" - as long as it is *evidence* that we pluck from daily life, the "love issue" is never settled, the "case" never closed. Why is this true? Why is it that *in the courtroom* the profound truth of God's love for us never really sinks in? We need to be clear about the answers to that question.

First, as we have seen, in the courtroom everything comes as evidence. This blocks the reception of God's love because the Father's love cannot be received as a verdict that we render based upon evidence weighed on the scales of justice. It can only be received by the one who is free to release love into the depths of his or her heart and mind. But this never happens with evidence; evidence can only be weighed. New evidence? Different verdict!

Second, the "love issue" can never be settled in a courtroom because only God's perfect love can set us free and that perfect love *is inseparable from his perfect truth.* What does this have to do with the courtroom? Simply this: when we occupy God's throne of judgement our little self-serving "truth" sits there in the place of God's perfect Truth! When we occupy that throne we turn from child-like trust in the one who is the truth to ask Pilot's question, *"What is truth?"* [John 18:38]. So, when we occupy the judgement seat we cannot avoid viewing "truth" cynically. As a false judge, truth can never be an absolute for us: it is "made by hand" in the ever changing shape of a thing which serves the fleeting purposes of the moment [*see* Isaiah 44:9-20]. So we see the utterly disastrous consequence of our courtroom idolatry: in the courtroom we cannot know the love our heart longs for because *perfect (absolute) love cannot be known apart from perfect (absolute) truth.*

Third, the "case" can never be closed in our courtroom because only mercy can overcome the judgement we live under [James 2:13] and there is no mercy available there. The only "place" where we can receive the mercy we need is at the feet of the one who has all authority and who *is* mercy - from the only Righteous Judge as he (and he alone) sits on the judgement seat of our hearts. There at his feet we are in a position to understand the depths of his unconditional love because it comes in the form of his gift of scandalous mercy: *"I have not come to judge you but to save you"* [John 12:47]. Only when we have been set free from idolatry by the power of the shed blood of the judge, are we able to receive both the giver and the gift of love.

But there is one more major road block to receiving God's love and to living from our identity as a child of God. We need to examine that in more detail; though it has been there in much of what has been said, we have not dealt directly with this deep inner resistance. We will look at it closely now.

Resistance to love and truth

"Answers" at the core: lies received

As we have seen, profound questions (especially concerning our personal identity) are there in the hearts of all who live in the courtroom. We gather evidence concerning those things, but what we need to consider now is this: *evidence seldom comes to us in a void.* Right there in our hearts, alongside *questions* about our identity (and today's evidence concerning it) are *"answers"* that have come to us during our life-time - very strong evidence, if you will, that we grip, and that grips us - most especially "answers" that come to us in childhood and remain with us.

As vulnerable children we receive a great deal of information from adults - especially from our parents - *about who we are*. The things parents say to us - the way we are treated, responded to, etc - all of this comes to us as "truth" about us. If I am constantly getting messages from my father that no matter how hard I try, no matter what I do or don't do, I cannot please him, I end up believing something about myself based on that "authoritative" word. This happens because as a child I do not have the physical, mental, emotional or spiritual recourses to put any distance between this powerful adult's word and my own heart and mind. When I am little, I accept what "big people" say as truth. If they tell me the moon is made of cheese, then it is. If they tell me that Santa slides down the chimney and up again, I believe it. Period. (Until Hilary, with the "no nonsense" parents, plants doubt during break.)

It would be a mistake to underestimate the power of the things we take in as children; these "messages" can be, literally, curses that we carry in us all our lives, acknowledged or not. On the one hand, there sometimes *is* awareness: many adults *consciously* believe lies about themselves received in childhood. If asked what he or she thinks of themselves, one such person might say something like "I'm not worth the space I take up or the air I breathe!" I have heard that exact self-judgement more than once ... *from Christians*. The person probably doesn't go around broadcasting this daily - they may put up an effective front much of the time - but underneath they believe it. Such a person may not want to believe it - they may understand that it makes no sense rationally and that it certainly does not square with their faith - but they do believe it and they are in touch with that fact. Any "evidence" they receive to the contrary (even the Gospel) fights a losing battle with this fundamental self-judgement.

On the other hand, I may be completely unaware that I have beliefs about who I am that lie beneath the surface. Having been received by me in childhood, these "messages" or "answers" are now beliefs I have about myself which have a huge impact on how I view the world and especially on how I relate to myself, others and God. I act and react not as the person I think I am or ought to be, but rather as the child I was: a deceived child, held in the powerful grip of a lie.

This is how it was for Karen. Throughout her childhood Karen learned that "love" only comes as a reward for perfect performance. The experience of being loved and accepted came rarely for her and evaporated quickly. The bottom line was that she lived with lies about who she was. These messages functioned as "answers" to the questions "Who am I? Am I loved? Am I loveable?" As an adult, Karen searched for love - for evidence that she was "worthy" of love (an oxymoron if ever there was one) - but the power of the words deep in her ("You do not deserve love"!) - received on many different levels and over the course of many years - severely undermined the power of the love she had, in fact, experienced and tried to receive. Karen was far from unique in this.

"Answers" at the core: curses spoken

There is another aspect to our development that we need to consider. Children are not just passive in relation to the circumstances and experiences of their lives. Two children may be exposed to essentially the same environment including shared parents, etc., but the effects on them very likely differ. We are shaped not just by the things that happen to us, but by a number of other factors and most crucially by *our response* to the things that happen to us.

Sometimes a child responds to the behaviour of a parent by judging him or her. While this judgement is seldom conscious and often very "understandable", in that it comes from a real experience of objectively destructive behaviour, it is an act of the will and it does lead to consequences be they ever so unforeseeable and unintended. If I walk the forest in ignorance of the danger around me and am attacked by a bear, my ignorance and lack of intention does not change the fact that I have to deal with the bear. In the same way, if, as a child, I enter into bitter judgement of a parent, I live with the devastating effect of that judgement. Until and unless I renounce the curse my heart has spoken, I live under that curse.

The warning contained in the fifth commandment implies that children do not stand apart from the law of sowing and reaping, especially in their relationship with parents. Paul reminds the Ephesians of the commandment (*"Honour your father and mother .... that it may go well with you ..."*), but goes on to warn fathers, in particular, that they need to be careful not to incite their children to become "exasperated" [more literally, that they do not *"rouse to wrath"*; Ephesians 6:1-4; see Deut 5:16]. Behind Paul's exhortation lies his awareness of potentially damaging consequences for the child. A child's response to his or her father and mother matters, *for good or ill*. But Paul warns fathers that they bear some responsibility for those consequences when they present the child with more than they are able to handle. He acknowledges the fact that we can, in effect, tempt a child to bitter judgement beyond that child's ability to resist.

What are the consequences in later life for a child who makes a bitter judgement against a parent? Here is the witness of Susan (*not her real name*) who, as a young girl, made a strong and bitter judgement of her mother and father as "bad parents". Given the way judgement works, what would we expect to see in this person's life as an adult? Simply this: we would expect that in the same way she judged her parents, she would be judged! By whom? By herself and consequently, by everyone else too. Susan's childhood judgement hung like a sword over her own life as a parent. This is her description of her adult experience:

"I have always looked up to my friend, Beth. She has firm convictions and is very proactive when it comes to parenting. I have always compared myself to her and found myself lacking. Whenever I would visit her we would share all that we were learning about the Lord, relationships, etc. When it came to parenting, I would share my struggles with her and she would give me advice. Her advice always left me feeling inadequate. I would see how well behaved her children were, how they were so helpful, didn't complain when told to do something, were very responsible ... the list went on. I looked at my kids and all I saw was how I was failing as a parent. They didn't have those same qualities to the same degree. Then my poor children would have to put up with my reactive behaviour after the visit. I'd want to whip them into shape and have them behaving like Beth's children within a week. I was very frustrated and they must have been resentful of all the expectations placed on them. I still do this to some degree. I hear of another child's great accomplishment and I wonder if I've done a poor job with my kids because they don't do the same things."

While it was true that the judgement Susan lived under did have an effect on her children and on her relationship with them, it was also true that she had many wonderful ways with them - she gave them many gifts, including the gift of herself. Her children did have experience of unconditional love from her because she was able to offer a measure of the love she had received from God.

But this fuller truth was often lost on Susan, because "evidence" about her competence as a parent did not enter a void. She lived under the judgement she had made of her parents as a girl, turned back on herself: "I am a bad mother". The jury was stacked!

A verdict was already in! She was hypersensitive to any evidence that she was a "bad parent" and she lived with the guilt, shame and self-loathing such evidence never failed to stir up in her. Did that evidence carry the same weight as evidence of her *good* parenting? Absolutely not! Was it a fair fight? No! "Good parent" evidence was a light weight challenger going up against a heavy weight champion: "bad parent" evidence could afford to swagger into the ring knowing that it packed the knockout punch of a judgement made long ago.

"Answers" at the core: "magical thinking"

During a time of prayer, Henry remembered being about 5 years old. One day his father came home from work and pulled into the driveway. He had to slam on his brakes because Henry had left his tricycle there in the drive. In a fury, his father got out of the car and began to yell at Henry who had run up to greet him.

"What's wrong with you? How many times have I told you not to leave your bike in the driveway?!" Intense adult anger hit him in the face from close range: "But it doesn't matter to you, does it? Does it?! You just go ahead and leave your junk all over the place, even though I've told you time after time after time! But you don't listen, do you?! Why can't you just do what you're told to do? What's wrong with you?!" On and on he went. When he was through, he stormed into the house.

The next morning Henry's father left for work and never returned. Henry knew the reason why his father had left home. It was because of him; it was because Henry had left his tricycle in the driveway.

As a child I view myself as the "centre of the universe". All things revolve around me. I am the cause of all that happens in my world. I want my baseball hero to get a hit and when he does, right on cue, I know it's because I was rooting for him. If I yell at the cat who then gets hit by a car, I was somehow the cause of his death. If my parents fight, it's because I was bad. Henry lived with the consequences of this kind of "magical thinking" long after he grew up.

For many years Henry lived with the sense that when things did not go well at work or at home he was the cause of it. Even though this was seldom a conscious thought, he lived with a steady, low-level anxiety which pressed him down. He was a faithful, prayerful man of God and knew a measure of "the joy of the Lord", and yet a depressing heaviness could descend on him in a flash. He didn't know why little everyday things could be so devastating. An offhand remark by his wife could fill him with shame and guilt: "Henry, your brother called to say that he finally had to take Judy to the hospital this afternoon. By the way, did you remember to pray for her this morning?" His daughter's minor disappointment could cut him like a knife and fill him with sadness: "Why did you come home so late, daddy? Now we can't go to the park!"

Make no mistake, as an adult he knew it had not been his fault that his father had left home. But inside lived a little boy who still believed the lie and the deep well of sadness, shame and guilt that had filled him as a child continued to overflow into his mind and heart until he was well into his 40's - until Jesus meet him there as his Saviour, Healer and Judge! The critical turning came only when the fundamental work was done. No matter how much genuine healing he received, it was only when Henry received the grace to stop judging himself that he was set free. Filled at last with overwhelming mercy, he was able to receive and release into his own mind and heart the precious gift he so desperately needed. The gift did not - could not - come in the courtroom of human rebellion. It did not come as evidence. The absolute truth of the Father's love for him came to him in the only place it could come: at the feet of the only Righteous Judge.

Provision and purpose as evidence

We have seen how love - even God's love - comes as evidence in our courtroom. Evidence about whether or not I'm loved is, of course, evidence about *who I am* - about my identity. Our search for love is inseparable from our search for our lost identity because the truth of God's love is the foundation of that identity. It remains for us to consider the other major areas of human loss: provision and purpose.

As we have said, the roots of our anxiety about provision and purpose lie in the loss of the identity for which we were created, but while the deepest issue is always identity, for some of us the circumstances of our lives (and our response to those circumstances!) result in a particular sensitivity to evidence that we are not safe and/or that our life has no meaning.

So far as life in the courtroom goes, the key with provision and purpose is the same as it was with identity; first and foremost, everything that happens in our courtroom comes as evidence. Evidence that I *am* safe, that I *do* have enough of the necessities of life and that my life *does* have meaning and purpose--all of this, when it comes, is weighed but cannot be received into the heart. As a result, neither the "provision issue" nor the "purpose issue" is ever settled; neither "case" is ever closed.

All that we have said about the various kinds of resistance we have to receiving love and truth can be applied to provision and purpose. One example will suffice.

If I grew up in a family that experienced deprivation and fear resulting from a severe economic depression, I may have an "answer" about provision at the core of my being. As an adult, if I get a raise in pay that "evidence" about my provision does not come to me in a void! I live with a "default" answer to the question: "Am I economically safe?" The answer may be something like this: *"No, I am not safe! Just when you think you're safe everything gets swept away in a minute! That's the way it is in this world"* This answer carries more weight than any material provision I may accumulate in later life. It is a preoccupation of my heart. I am particularly sensitive to evidence in this area and prone to anxiety about it.

But the question might be asked, "Is this really judgement?" The most important thing to consider here is that this example is not simply a description of someone who reasonably acknowledges some truth: *"Everything material, including my material provision, could, in fact, get swept away in a minute! If some economic event or 'natural' disaster comes my way I may experience severe loss and hardship. Such things might even result in my death, especially if combined with the action or inaction of sinful human institutions and systems."* To understand this and to take some reasonable preparations and precautions in the face of it is neither faithless nor the outworking of destructive judgement.

But the above example is altogether different: it has the ear marks of bondage to judgement. It sounds like the person is reaping a crop of fear - fear with bitterness mixed in. If fear and bitterness are what is being reaped, what was sown? Judgement, yes, but against whom or what? There are several possibilities. First, it might be self-judgement. Perhaps a curse that goes something like this: "I will never be safe!" It might be more directly about identity: "I am not worth protecting!"

But we need to consider another possibility: this example may indicate judgement applied in an arena we have not considered up until now. If we live in the courtroom our judgement will be exercised in all our relationships: in our relationship with others, including God (*inter*personal), in our relationship with ourselves (*intra*personal) and in the relationship we have with groups of people (inter-social). This last category may apply here. It is not at all uncommon for us to judge whole cultures, nations, governments, races, organizations and so on. In the example we are looking at, it might be that a judgement has been made against "the world". Perhaps a major theme in this person's family as he or she grew up was: "Good things happen to others, but not to us. As soon as we manage to get anything the roof falls in and it's all gone." The judgement - spoken or unspoken - might go something like this: "The world is against us!" We might notice in passing that this judgement reflects a not-so-subtle form of "magical thinking": "I am (we are) the centre of the universe!" "Because of me (us) the tornado came!"

Beyond the courtroom

Paul: out of the judgement business?

> " *I care very little if I am judged by you or by any human court; indeed, I do not even judge myself. My conscience is clear, but that does not make me innocent. It is the Lord who judges me. Therefore judge nothing before the appointed time; wait till the Lord comes. He will bring to light what is hidden in darkness and will expose the motives of men's hearts.*" [1 Corinthians 4:3-5]

Is Paul just "whistling in the dark?" Is the statement "*I care very little if I am judged by you or by any human court*" an example of the defensive bragging we described in chapter six ("*... [one] strategy might involve my projecting the attitude that I couldn't care less what anyone thinks of me.*")? If we took this one opening phrase in isolation, it might indicate exactly that: we could imagine it as a defensive ploy, delivered by someone looking down his nose at us with a sneer.

On the other hand, the second phrase doesn't lend itself so easily to that picture; he says he doesn't judge himself. This added to the first phrase and taken completely at face value could look like the profile of someone who is "out of the judgement business."

But if we acknowledge that arrogance could have informed the first phrase, why not the second: "I do not even judge myself"? He may not mean this literally at all. What if he only means that he finds nothing in himself to condemn? Paul may be dispensing that old courtroom counterfeit of God's mercy: the courtroom judgement of himself as "innocent"!

The tables of evidence gathering overturned:

But now as Paul continues on in verse four all our speculation is blown away: "*My conscience is clear, but that does not make me innocent. It is the Lord who judges me.*" There is no more profound witness in all the scriptures to a life freed from the bondage of judgement. Just as Paul threw away a righteousness that he once valued, based on keeping the law, as though it was rubbish [Philippians 3:4-9], so now he discards a counterfeit of God's mercy that would be based on a clear conscience. *Paul doesn't regard the content of his conscience as evidence to be weighed*: he is out of the weighing business. He is not trying to secure anything for himself. Paul is now in the business of losing everything he had gained for himself in the old life. The only thing he wants to "gain" now is Christ!

Paul has given up everything for the sake of a pearl; all the legacy of human loss has been restored to Paul in the "pearl" of the kingdom [Matthew 13:45f]: Christ his Saviour, Lord and only Judge!

The foundation is a restored identity. Having been "found in Christ", Paul knows who he is: a child of God - a "son" [Romans 8:15f]! As a "son" Paul knows who the judge is: his Saviour, the Son of God. So Paul is not pretending that he doesn't care about the judgement that comes from other people; he actually doesn't care! Not in an arrogant way. There is no sneer - just the simple truth spoken in the freedom that comes from the One who now sits on the judgement seat in Paul's heart. The Lord, and only the Lord, judges him. Because he does not judge himself, the judgement of others has no power in him: there is no place in him to receive it.

I find this passage almost overwhelming: here is the essential core of this "Courtroom" teaching, freeze-dried. Paul exposes the heart of it all in a few words. This is amazing, incredible, awesome and ... well ... a little irritating. At least I pretend sometimes that I am offended. It's a little joke I have going with the Judge. But the Father knows the truth: I am grateful for this word of life; for this word of living hope. Paul got out of the judgement business by the grace of God! I am inspired (I hope you are too) to move on - to move out and to move in by that same grace!

Where we go from here: moving out and moving in!

Most of us would honestly (and could truthfully) say that both our parenting and our parents' parenting was a mixed bag: there are godly and ungodly aspects to the heritage we have received and passed on. The fact that we have lived with judgement and that it has infected our relationships is a truth we must deal with, but it is not the only truth.

As this discussion of life in the courtroom draws to a close it will be good to acknowledge that for many of us it has not been judgement only that we have known: the grace of God has come to us from parents (and/or others) who loved, protected, nurtured and guided us with at least a measure of the goodness, wisdom and love of God. For some this has been by God's grace, consciously known in some measure. For others this has happened simply because the Father is at work. We have received a gift without knowing we received anything at all, from the hand of an, as yet, unknown giver.

We turn our eyes now toward "The Father's House". As we go forward seeking to leave the courtroom behind just as Paul did - to get out of the idolatry business and receive Jesus as our judge - we will need faith and courage to pay whatever it costs - to lose whatever it is we need to lose; to die to whatever we need to die to - in order that we may live effectively in and from the identity that was the Father's will for us in creation: "Child of God." What would encourage us? I submit that the best encouragement is the truth affirmed! I invite you to affirm this truth in prayer before going on:

Father, I seek now to leave the courtroom more completely behind, taking hold of the one who has come to set me free. I believe that your love and your truth will be built up in me. Where judgement has lived, I believe that love will have a home. The stronghold of deception in me will weaken and fall and your stronghold of Truth will strengthen and rise. The cursing and death I have sown and which cries out in me will be silenced by the cry of the only righteous Judge - the crucified Son!

I believe that Jesus reaped the judgement I sowed so that I can reap the blessing and the life he sowed for my sake. The place in me that has welcomed condemnation will give way to a great and mighty flood of your mercy, Father. I will no longer seek to take by force what you desire to give me by grace. Lord Jesus, take your throne in me: I will receive the Father's mercy at your feet. Come Holy Spirit, cleanse my heart. Fill me with the Father's love; fill me with the Father's will; fill me with all Truth; fill me with the heart's cry of the Beloved: "Abba, Father!"

BOOK TWO:

THE FATHER'S HOUSE

Introduction

His purpose

Because he loves us, the Father tells us the truth: we can't have him plus a few other gods as backup in case things aren't going as well as we would like them to! The truth is that in every kind of circumstance - when things seem to be going well and when they don't - God "works for the good of those who love him, who have been called according to his purposes [Romans 8:29]." The "gods" (idols) we hedge our bets with do not work for our good though they may promise to work for our ease. They promise to provide an easy road today but they lead us into a deep pit tomorrow. In contrast, the Living God offers truth: his "narrow way" is a harder road today. But he walks with us on that road and leads us into righteousness, peace and joy tomorrow, and the day after, and forever. The bottom line is this: *God is on "our side."* He wants the very best for us. He is patient when we stray; he seeks us when we are lost. When he finds us he carries us home with joy. But he says "go and stray no more." [John 8:11] Why? Because he hates sin. And why does God hate sin? Because he loves sinners.

He has demonstrated that love in Jesus. There is no hill of idolatry so lofty that he cannot ascend to bring us down where we ought to be. Jesus has paid the price so that he can come there to us. There is no pit of pain and hopelessness so deep that he cannot come down to us and lift us up. Jesus spent himself to make that possible too. On the cross he opened up the way of salvation to the arrogant heights and the despairing depths of our sinful, lost humanity. So we see that this love that we refer to - God's love - is an active investment of himself.

It is this personally invested love that is the motive behind the commandment, "You shall have no other gods before me ..." God tells us that it was from jealousy that he gave us this first commandment [Exodus 20:3-5b], but his jealousy is as unlike our jealousy as his judgement is unlike our judgement. God knows that for us it is either his life or no life. So the commandment issues from the deepest place of his love: he is jealous for the sake of life for us.

It is from the well of his jealous, unconditional love that Jesus speaks to us about our judgement: "Unless I am your only Judge, I am not your only Lord." These were his words to me. He did not need to say more to me or to you. If he is not our only Lord, then what? Then he is not our only life, or mediator, or Saviour. Unless God is our only Judge, he is not our only God. These can be disturbing words. They should be. They were spoken to shake us. They are released to shake the Church. But they are the source of new hope. First, because after God's shaking only his life will remain. Second, because when his word opens our eyes we finally see and know something fundamental about what has held us back as we have tried to live as his children...as his Body! The idol that lies behind our resistance to the growth of obedient life in us has been unveiled. What a shock this is: we have met the judge and he is us! When the veil is parted, we stand exposed. But he does not shame us. He is kind and merciful. He covers us with his word: "Let me be for you what you cannot be for yourself. In me there is no condemnation."

If the Lord has been inviting us to see the courtroom more clearly it is for the sake of establishing freedom in us - a freedom for which he has set us free [Galatians 5:1]. It is his desire to arrange a meeting between his mercy and our judgement. I believe that Jesus desires to come into the courtroom of our hearts in order to bring us out and then to bring us in: in to the place of eternal life he is building in us - into his Father's house. If we welcome him and begin to see as he sees, we will see beyond the old life of bondage in the courtroom to free and abundant life as children of the Father. In his Son, by the Holy Spirit, the Father has sown his love in us, so we know that our hope of freedom will not disappoint: in Jesus, the Father has been and done all that is necessary so that we can live with him now and forever as sons and daughters.

His revelation

Jesus said "If you have seen me, you have seen the Father" [John 14:9]. I believe it is also true that if we have seen him in his perfect humanness, we have seen a revelation of ourselves as we were created to be: *he walked this earth living the humanity that was ours in creation!* When we see him in the light of truth - in other words, as we see him in the scriptures and as he is personally with us - we cannot fail to notice that there is a qualitative distance between us. But there is Good News: a way to bridge the distance. Jesus himself is the Way: the one road from here to there. He is the only Way to the Father and *he is the Way to that true humanity whose life is with the Father* [John 14:1-7]. In other words, Jesus doesn't leave us where he found us: Jesus is the way from who we are to who he is.

It has been said before: he became like us so that we could become like him: the second Adam [1 Corinthians 15:45-49]. The completion of the Father's plan for us entails the restoration of our humanity as we are "conformed to the likeness of his Son" [Romans 8:29]. Eternal life does not mean the rejection or loss of our humanity, but its perfection.

His parables

The perfect picture of divinity and humanity that comes to us in the person of Jesus also comes in his teaching. Especially in the parables, both aspects of his revelation (human and divine) are apparent. *First* he shows us the Father. Again and again in the parables we see snap shots of the Father's will, his ways and his heart. Jesus speaks to us about what the Father loves and what he hates.

Second, as he tells stories of ordinary and not so ordinary men and women, Jesus unveils the human heart. We see faith, loyalty and humble repentance. But we also see brokenness, fear, arrogance, unfaithfulness, deceit, hypocrisy ... we see judgement in all its guises.

The condition of our hearts - the destructive life of bondage we lead in the courtroom - does not change the Father's heart. After all, it was for the sake of our captive hearts that the Righteous Judge entered our courtroom in the first place. He came to set the captives free. He came to make it possible for us to be *in* the courtroom of this world but not *of* it. This becomes possible as Jesus leads us out of our personal courtrooms into the house where children of the Father live with him in freedom.

His path

The rest of this book comes with an invitation to undertake a journey "out" and "in" with Jesus. A chapter will be devoted to each of three parables; they are Jesus' provision for us as we go with him: Living Bread to nourish us on his Way. We will hear about the owner of a vineyard, a king and a father. We will hear of workers hired in that vineyard, of the king's servant upon whom extravagant mercy is poured and of two wayward sons of a father who desires that both his sons be with him and enter into his joy.

In each chapter we will learn from Jesus about the Father's heart and ours. We will see the truth of who he is and who we are through personal, contemporary witness. In prayer we will have the opportunity to offer ourselves to Jesus and to receive him as he comes in love and truth as the only Righteous Judge, to set us free.

†

Chapter 10

The Workers In The Vineyard

The scandal of the Father's grace

The parable

Matthew 20

[1] *"For the kingdom of heaven is like a landowner who went out early in the morning to hire men to work in his vineyard. [2] He agreed to pay them a denarius for the day and sent them into his vineyard.*

[3] *"About the third hour he went out and saw others standing in the marketplace doing nothing. [4] He told them, 'You also go and work in my vineyard, and I will pay you whatever is right.' [5] So they went.*

"He went out again about the sixth hour and the ninth hour and did the same thing. [6] About the eleventh hour he went out and found still others standing around. He asked them, 'Why have you been standing here all day long doing nothing?'

[7] *"'Because no one has hired us,' they answered.*

"He said to them, 'You also go and work in my vineyard.'

8 "When evening came, the owner of the vineyard said to his foreman, 'Call the workers and pay them their wages, beginning with the last ones hired and going on to the first.'

9 "The workers who were hired about the eleventh hour came and each received a denarius. 10So when those came who were hired first, they expected to receive more. But each one of them also received a denarius. 11When they received it, they began to grumble against the landowner. 12 'These men who were hired last worked only one hour,' they said, 'and you have made them equal to us who have borne the burden of the work and the heat of the day.'

13 "But he answered one of them, 'Friend, I am not being unfair to you. Didn't you agree to work for a denarius? 14Take your pay and go. I want to give the man who was hired last the same as I gave you. 15Don't I have the right to do what I want with my own money? Or are you envious because I am generous?'

Reflection: "That's just like me"

"Is this fair? Is this just? Am I getting what I deserve? Is someone getting more than they deserve?" As the day's wages are being distributed, these are likely the questions that fill the hearts and minds of the workers hired early. They are symptoms that rise up in anyone who has the experience of being "offended." That is what these workers have experienced: they have been offended by the actions of the owner of the vineyard.

One of the most universal and commonly occurring human experiences is that of being "offended". Whole systems of social convention grow up around the attempt to avoid giving offence. Perhaps for that reason it would never occur to most of us that there is anything wrong with *being* offended. It is the one who gives offence (the offender) who is in the wrong! But, while it certainly may be true that a person who is being "offensive" may have "issues", there is no avoiding the simple truth: if I *receive* that offence - if I *become offended* - I am in the courtroom! The preoccupations of our hearts and minds when we are offended look, taste, feel and sound like destructive judgement because they are judgement ... every time.

When we become offended, a judge literally lifts up in us. One can actually feel that "person" - that judge - rising up internally! The symptoms may very well be external too: our chin lifts; our eyes widen in haughty, self-righteousness. We swell up like a toad. We wear the offence like a garment. We begin to "grumble" even if we are by ourselves. We put on our robe and take the bench: an injustice has been committed and there is a case to be made (the grumbling *is the sound of a case being made*). Assemble all the corroborating witnesses that can be found; bring on the evidence - stack up every deeply satisfying piece of it! But the verdict is in before the hearing begins. We wear a sneer as we deliver the judgement. We drip contempt because the delicious poison is already leaking out into our mind and heart; it burns through us as we make our list with the help of those around us:

They came late because they knew it would be cooler!

They only worked one lousy little hour!

I did most of the real work and they got a full day's wage! Unbelievable!

The owner wouldn't know justice if he got his head caught in it!

He acts like all my hard labour is worth the same as their piddling little bit of so-called "work"!

The longer the list grows the better, the more justified, the more righteous *and the more offended* we feel. All the elements of the legal world are in place. It's a clear cut case: we are innocent! They are guilty! The whole world should know and proclaim the purity and righteousness of our cause and stand with us in the face of this insulting injustice!

Sometimes the offending party is a vineyard owner; sometimes a father or mother; sometimes the deacon, the coach, a brother or "that woman he married". In full awareness, Jesus tells the story and invites us to look closely: "That's just like you", he says. "Yes", we say. "Yes, it is. But not just *like* me. That *is* me!"

Witness: "That is me!"

"That's not fair"

A few years ago, the opportunity presented itself for me to go into full-time ministry. I had been seeking God's direction and felt led to go into hospital chaplaincy. I applied for an internship at a large hospital about an hour from my home. The pastoral staff described themselves as "interfaith" and the training programme was open to people of every faith.

Once I was accepted into the programme, I learned that the commitment would be one day a week spent in "group" time, two spent on the hospital floors doing visitations, and twice a month I would have to do a 24 hour on-call with the entire time spent at the hospital answering calls to deaths, codes, traumas, and emergencies along with the floor visitations. Most of these on-calls were done on weekends. If I had a Sunday on-call, it was followed immediately by my Monday group time which meant I was at the hospital 34 hours usually with no sleep. It was challenging emotionally and physically, but I knew what I was committing to up-front.

One of the interns was a pastor named Jerry. This man was very liberal in his thinking. During our group time, it became obvious that I was an orthodox Christian - one who was at the opposite end of the theological spectrum from Jerry.

Once in our group time we were told that we were expected to encourage patients in their faith no matter what their faith was. We had just heard an example of a psychiatric patient who was a Wiccan or "white witch" and desired a knife and a candle so she could worship. I spoke up and said I had a problem with that. I could receive the person, but I wouldn't encourage someone in something I believed would be dangerous to her. Jerry attacked me, calling me judgemental, and another ordained Christian minister told me Christianity was more dangerous than Wicca. From that point on I felt like I was targeted and persecuted. Everything I said was challenged. I didn't feel a part of this group, and I really wanted to quit the programme, but my supervisor said there was plenty of room for an orthodox Christian and asked me to stay. I did because I loved ministering on the floor. It gave me a chance to be with people as Jesus was with them . I felt that this was truly what God was calling me to.

Then one day I heard Jerry say he didn't have to do the 24 hour on-call times because it would be too conflicting with his Sunday obligation of preaching. He couldn't do a Saturday since he needed to prepare his sermons, and Sunday he would be preaching. I already knew he didn't have to work the two days on the floor because he had pastoral visitations with parishioners. But so did I! It had been my position as pastoral assistant in the church that qualified me for the chaplaincy programme. I thought, "He's getting special treatment because they want his type. That's it. They say this programme is open to all faiths, but I'm constantly put down and Jerry doesn't ever have to go out on the hospital floor. That's not fair."

Why did I have to travel an hour those other two days? I made several pastoral visits every week. Jerry couldn't miss Sunday to do on-call, but what about the rest of us? We all had responsibilities at our churches. Besides that, they were all against me. They didn't like me. I had all the evidence. Articles were being posted in the department that I assumed were there to better educate me about gay marriages, etc. I believed they were whispering behind my back about the position our church was taking on some issues that were highly publicized. They all knew of the church I attended and where I held a position of leadership. They said all faiths were acceptable, but orthodox Christianity seemed to be the one exception. I needed to quit. How could I continue? Jerry was getting to go through the programme without doing *the work. The only thing he had to do was come to the group time and harass me. He was getting the same credit for the internship as I was without doing what was required. I didn't care if I lost my tuition money and the credit. I was about to quit. It just wasn't fair.*

Then Jesus brought the parable of the "workers in the vineyard" to me.

The Way Out

Reflection: "That's just like my Father"

Jesus tells us that the parable of the workers in the vineyard is about the kingdom of God, so we know that when he talks about the vineyard owner he is teaching about God the Father. We see the owner of the vineyard primarily in relation to two groups of people: those who have been there working all day and those who come to his service "late in the day". We have seen that the early workers are offended by the owner. According to them the offence is a lack of fairness in the distribution of wages. They rely on a legalistic point: the owner gives equal pay for *un*equal work. The owner disposes of their claim by reminding them of the fact that he has fulfilled the terms of their agreement. Then he points to their hearts. He says, in effect, "This isn't really about your wages, is it? You know as well as I that at the start of the day you knew this to be a fair wage, and you know it's still fair at the end of the day. That's not really why you're offended. You're jealous, aren't you? These men got more than they earned and you didn't: it was my generosity to them that offends you!"

Few would anticipate having any problem with a God who is merciful and generous - who blesses lavishly. Surely we would be filled with thankfulness to see our great God demonstrating his great goodness. But Jesus strips away our illusions. The Father's generosity is often perceived as a miscarriage of justice to us. Sometimes others get more than we do. We respond to this as though it is a threat to our wellbeing! And it *is* a threat if we believe we are in charge of providing for ourselves. If we don't stick up for ourselves, making sure that we get everything we have a "right" to or "deserve", then who will? God's generosity can also be a threat to our identity. If "they" got more than I got, what does that say about me? Am I not worth as much as they? Does he love them more than he loves me? What's wrong with me? "Offences" are items of information received in the heart of a judge who gathers and weighs evidence.

In Jesus' parable we see the truth about who the Father really is: he keeps his promises. He is faithful. But he is also generous. It pleases him to pour out mercy and kindness. This is the very best thing there could be for us as it fits our situation perfectly. The wages we have worked for and earned are the wages of sin. But Jesus reveals the source of our hope: it is the Father's joy to give us the gift of life in his kingdom [Luke 12:32]. Like all God's gifts this is something we don't deserve and can't earn. This can be offensive to the one who has worked all day and who insists that everyone get what they deserve. If we insist, the Father will hand out the payment we have earned. But he prefers to give gifts because that is what love does and that is what we need.

Witness: That *is* my Father! Witness of truth spoken in love.

"That's Not Fair", Part II

> *When I read the words of Jesus in the parable of the workers in the vineyard, I realized that I really had no ground to stand on. I was grumbling about a*

decision that was none of my business. What did that decision made about Jerry have to do with me? I knew what my commitments would be up-front and agreed to them. I felt persecuted, but what about the call to the ministry? Did I want to enter into what God was calling me to? The only way out of this struggle was going to mean death to my flesh. I knew I wasn't the judge. Jesus was making that very clear to me. Jesus, the righteous judge says, "Anyone who does not take his cross and follow me is not worthy of me. Whoever finds his life will lose it, and whoever loses his life for my sake will find it. He who receives you receives me, and he who receives me receives the one who sent me." Didn't I know that following Him was going to cost me something? A servant is not above his Master. Jesus meant it when he said: he was sending me out as a sheep among wolves. Following Him was not about being comfortable and accepted.

I needed to come off the judgement seat where I was giving power to others to tell me if I was acceptable or valuable I had to ask God to forgive me and invite Him to be my judge. I also needed to forgive Jerry for having hurt me and the others for having offended me.

God filled my heart with his mercy and I offered it to those who were persecuting me. I stayed on the programme and asked God to teach me the truth about myself even through these folks who seemed to be against me. Through his grace I could love them and live in truth. In God's mercy, I could hear what had seemed to be attacks and listen with Jesus to see if there was any truth spoken which I could benefit from even if it didn't come in a pretty package. I committed myself to hearing the truth no matter how it came.

Four months after the programme began, we had a mid-term evaluation which included an in-depth description of our relationship with each person in the programme. For the brave at heart, this was a time for telling the truth. I told Jerry he hurt me many times by rejecting me and ridiculing my beliefs. I went on to say that I lived with the fear that if he knew who I truly was, he would fully reject me. I also affirmed him in many ways. Amazingly enough, I had learned many things about myself from Jerry, so I let him know how much I valued his input. I told Jerry I valued him.

The truth came to him as a gift. All of a sudden he saw me as a person - one he had hurt. The love and mercy I had shown him melted his heart. He began to weep and swooped me into his arms apologizing and asking for forgiveness.

He went on to say that he had grown up in the evangelical church where he was taught that he must remain chaste until marriage. Later, while in seminary, he rushed into marriage because he lusted. He wound up with a woman who made him miserable and the church told him divorce was not acceptable. He grew very depressed and went to see a therapist. The therapist told him to divorce, and Jerry rejected the teachings of the church and entered into what he

158

believed to be freedom. He thought God wanted him to be happy and grew to resent the church for imposing a bunch of stringent rules he believed had ruined his life. He thought God didn't like those rules either. He grew to hate the evangelical church and cursed it with profanities. I represented the church he hated, and his bitterness was slung at me.

I came to know that what Jerry said and did was simply an outpouring of what was in his heart. The judgement I experienced from him was truly given, but I didn't need to receive it. God was my judge. Because I was in judgement, I had wanted to quit. I wanted to flee, but by His grace, I was able to flee to the mercy of my Saviour Jesus.

Path Out of the Courtroom: with Jesus, looking at our hearts; receiving and responding to the Father's love expressed in truth.

A.

Questions: Have you seen a connection between receiving an offence and receiving judgement? Do you know from personal experience what it is like to wear an offence "like a garment"?

Love in Truth: Being "offended" is a sinful choice we make. We are called to confess the sin of that form of destructive judgement, to repent of it, and to seek the freeing, cleansing grace of God's forgiveness.

Prayer Path:
1. Ask Jesus to share the truth with you about any sinful habit patterns of "taking offence" that may exist in your life. Confess and repent of the sin of judgement called "being offended". Ask for and receive God's forgiveness.
2. Allow Jesus to bring to your mind specific persons who have "offended" you in the past. Confess and repent of the sinful judgement you embraced when you became "offended". Ask for and receive God's forgiveness.
3. Release to the care and love of Jesus all those who have "offended" you in the past. Bless each one in Jesus' name and pray that they and you will now be set free from any ill effects of your past judgement of them. If you believe anyone has judged you, ask Jesus to set you and them free of that same judgement by the merciful gift of his grace.

B.
Questions: Is Jesus your Lord? Is he Lord of all your life? Is he Lord of every relationship in your life?

Love in Truth: When we choose to judge by being offended by another person, we have excluded Jesus from the relationship we have with that person.

Prayer Path:
1. Lift up the relationships of your life to Jesus, including the one you have with yourself: invite him to come into the centre of each relationship as crucified and risen Lord.
2. Invite Jesus to come as your only mediator and separate you from anything which is not of him in all relationships.

3. Invite Jesus to come as reconciler and as the place of intimate meeting with others.
4. Speak to Jesus of your desire that you see yourself and others with his eyes and love as he loves.

The Way In

And what would things look like if we were conformed to the likeness of Jesus? What if the workers in the vineyard had the Father's heart? Just imagine...

Reflection: The Parable turned inside out!

Parable of the generous workers

For the kingdom of heaven is like a landowner who went out early in the morning to hire men to work in his vineyard. He offered them the usual wage of a denarius for the day and they accepted gladly. But one of the workers took him aside and said to him, "Sir, as we talked together this morning I discovered that one of us has a friend who is coming from a distance today to work. I want you to pay me less so that no matter when he comes you may pay him a full day's wage." The owner of the vineyard looking at the worker loved him. He agreed and the man went and worked all day.

About the third hour the owner went out and saw others standing in the marketplace doing nothing. He told them, "You also go and work in my vineyard, and I will pay you whatever is right." So they went. He went out again about the sixth hour and the ninth hour and did the same thing. About the eleventh hour the man came who had travelled a great distance. "Am I too late to work for you?" the man said. "There is still time," said the owner and sent the man into his fields to work.

When evening came, the owner of the vineyard said to his foreman, "Call the workers and pay them their wages, beginning with the last one hired and going on to the first." The worker who had been hired about the eleventh hour came and to his astonishment received a denarius. Quickly he found his friend who was waiting with the other workers. "Look!" he said, "the owner has given me a full day's wage though I only arrived an hour ago. How is this possible? Has he made a mistake?" "No mistake!" said his friend. And they all began to say to him, "It is no mistake! He has been generous that way with all of us!" And they rejoiced together.

The man hired early, who had come to speak with the owner of the vineyard, received the lesser wage he had agreed upon. Afterward he went to the owner and said "Thank you for allowing me to help that man." "You're welcome," said the owner. "I'm as happy as you are!" Then the owner and the worker went on their way rejoicing!

Witness: Just like him. Where we're going: witness of the Father's children.

When we begin to live as children of the Father, we become, in a very real sense, God's "word made flesh", just like Jesus. This is a wonderful thing because every time we "live his word" we open a way for that word to enter this sinful, broken world. Amazing things happen! This should come as no surprise. After all, the word we live out in our lives is the same mighty Word which brought all things into being - which created sun and seed, nebula and nucleus. So far as judgement goes, if, as sons and daughters of God, we embody the word "Do not judge", the power of the One who raised Jesus from the dead enters the place where we enter: our living room, the local grocery store, a church gathering...and when God's word is released through our obedient life, it does not return to him without accomplishing his purpose [Isaiah 55:11]. When the children of God glorify him, the parable of a judging world is turned upside down: the plan of the enemy is overturned, light comes into darkness, mercy flows like a river, the human heart is impacted by that for which the human heart was made.

Here is witness (by Rick Joyner) of one such outpouring. It is a great illustration of the fact that wherever his children are - even in an airport! - there the Father's word is active...

An airport hijacked

One of the greatest demonstrations of the Spirit I have ever witnessed was not a miracle, but a situation in an airline ticket line. Because of problems with incoming flights and other delays, the line to one connection had grown to many more people than could be processed in the short time before the flight was to depart. Strife and impatience were rising to the point where I seriously thought the situation was going to get out of control.

At the worst possible moment, just after more bad news had been announced, two large, boisterous women, each carrying two huge suitcases, started pushing their way through the line, demanding to go to the front. I do not recall ever witnessing more obnoxious attitudes. Even though they were women, I was fully expecting someone to deck them both. Then, to my dismay, they headed right toward my friend who was in line for the flight.

As others were actually beginning to jostle the two women, my friend instinctively raced to their assistance, asking if he could help them with their bags and offering them his own position near the front of the line. This action was so contrary to the prevailing spirit that everyone was stunned. A great quiet came over the entire scene. As my friend picked up his own bags and moved to the back of the line, every eye was on him. The two women were also undone by the unexpected, undeserved kindness.

The agents, who had also witnessed the scene, suddenly became agreeable and somehow the flight was delayed enough to get everyone on it. I have witnessed many miracles of biblical stature, but that airport scene still stands out to me as a profound demonstration of the kingdom. As hell was fast gaining control of a volatile situation, moving it toward potentially serious strife, Satan brought in two of his biggest guns and aimed them right at the Christian, who quickly disarmed the enemy and his entire host with one genuine act of kindness.

Path of the Father's Child. Freedom in the One who is truth: who we are; who he is; affirming the truth in prayer.

Questions: Can you remember a time when you were offended by someone? What was it, specifically, that offended you? Consider, with Jesus, how your response was related to your identity. What specific evidence were you gathering as you "gathered in" the offence? Who is your defender?

Love in Truth: Only the Lord can supply those things we are trying to secure for ourselves when we choose to be offended. In the simplest and deepest sense, what we need is this: to know the truth of who he is and who we are to him. We need to know and receive the truth Jesus brings and is. We need to release the truth into our own mind and heart.

Prayer path: Through prayer, affirm and give thanks for the truth who sets you free.

Abba Father: Prayer of Thanksgiving

Abba, Father: Thank you
> That you wanted me to be born
> That I don't have to be perfect for you to love me
> That I don't have to meet all your expectations to be loved
> That you *are* love for me

Abba, Father: Thank you
> That when I make mistakes, you do not turn away from me
> That when I fail, you do not love me any less
> That when I stray, you long for my return
> That when I confess my sin, you are always ready to forgive me

Abba, Father: Thank you
> That you delight in me as your child
> That you are perfectly aware of all that I need
> That you want what is best for me
> That you always provide what is best for me

Abba, Father: Thank you
> That you want me to know you
> That you want to really know me
> That you are always interested in me and in every part of my life
> That you are always faithful to me even when I am not faithful to you

Abba, Father: Thank you
> That you will never leave me
> That you will always be there to listen to me
> That you will always answer me
> That you are my Father and I am your child.

Chapter 11

The Unmerciful Servant:
A gift of debt rejected

The Parable [Matthew 18:21-35]

The Unmerciful Servant: A dramatization

King:	Who's next?
Bailiff:	Josephus, my lord.
King:	Bring him in.
Bailiff:	Yes, my lord.

(Bailiff leaves, returns leading Josephus)

King:	Do you know why you're here?
Josephus:	No, my lord.
King:	It's about your debt.
(To bailiff)	How much does he owe me?
Bailiff:	Six hundred and fifty trillion pounds, my lord.
Josephus:	O God! I can't pay it.
King:	Sell him to pay the debt.
Bailiff:	My lord, he's not worth that much.
Josephus:	O God!

King:	Sell his wife then.
Bailiff:	My lord, both of them together aren't worth that much.
Josephus:	O God!
King:	Sell his children too!
Bailiff:	My lord, I doubt the whole family is worth …
Josephus:	My lord, have mercy! Have patience and I'll find a way to pay you back!
King:	Take him away!
Josephus:	Lord! This is me! Josephus! Have mercy!
King:	Take him away!
Josephus:	Lord, think of my wife! Have mercy!
King:	Take him away!
Josephus:	Lord, think of my children!
King: *(to Bailiff)*	Wait!
(to Josephus)	I've heard your cry for mercy. It is my decision to cancel your whole debt.
(to Bailiff)	Cross his name off the books. He owes me nothing.
(to Josephus)	You're free. You may go!
Josephus:	
(as he leaves)	Thank you! Thank you! Thank you, my lord! Thank …
(*to fellow servant*)	You!
Fellow Servant:	What do you want, Joe?
Josephus:	You owe me six pounds, fifty!
Fellow Servant:	I can't pay it!
Josephus:	I want it all!
Fellow Servant:	Have patience. I'll find a way to pay you back!
Josephus:	I want it now!

Fellow Servant:	Have mercy!
Josephus:	*[to sheriff]* Sheriff! Arrest this man! Lock him up! Throw away the key!
Fellow Servant:	O God!

(Meanwhile, back at the castle ...)

King:	Yes. What is it?
Bailiff:	Lord. There's something you need to know about your servant Josephus.
King:	Tell me! *[The Bailiff whispers into his ear]* He didn't! *[more whispering]* He didn't! *[more whispering]* Bring him here! Bring him now!
King:	You are a wicked servant!
Josephus:	Lord, have mercy!
King:	No more begging. No more mercy. I cancelled that huge debt of yours but you've thrown your friend into prison for a few pence.
Josephus:	Mercy, lord!
King:	Mercy is wasted on you. You've chosen another way. Now you're going to grind your teeth in prison.
(to Bailiff)	Lock him up!
Bailiff:	Yes, my lord!
King:	And throw away the key!
Josephus:	O God!

Reflection: "That's just like me"

Josephus, our "unmerciful servant", appears to be in such a sorry state that one doubts his ability to offer any sort of "reflection" that would benefit us. As he "grinds his teeth" there in prison he is a mystery to himself. He does not know his own mind or heart. His sight is restricted to the "tunnel" vision characteristic of any of us when we are living in the tiny, close-walled cells of our idolatry. He looks at life with a desperate, self-serving squint, refusing to lift and open his eyes to the expansive, joy-filled world of the Father's mercy which surrounds him.

For a reflection on the condition of this servant's heart, we must look to those who know him:

King:

I don't understand. Why didn't my servant have any mercy for the other servant? He asked me for mercy. I examined my heart … and there it was! I gave it to him. And it seemed as though he took it.

But here's the thing: if I'd given him a hundred pounds here at court, then he'd have had a hundred pounds when he got out there on the street. But, even though I gave him mercy here, when he got to the other servant, he didn't have it any more. Where did it go?

Bailiff:

I think that Josephus wanted the benefits of the mercy - but he didn't want the mercy. Notice how he said "thank you." But what was he grateful for? I think he was only grateful because he didn't have to go to prison.

He was happy to take the benefits of the mercy - he was free to go - but he didn't want the mercy itself. So he didn't receive it. It's clear to me that if he had really received the mercy, then he would have had it to give his fellow servant. But you can't give away what you don't have.

Fellow Servant:

I agree. I know this guy. I know Joe. He's always got to have the upper hand. He wants leverage. He borrows because he can't stop spending. He got in way over his head this time because he just had to throw money around trying to buy friends and make things happen. He got so far in debt he never could have paid it back.

So how is it for a guy like Joe to have an un-payable debt forgiven? I'll tell you what it's like: he hates it! To him it's just another unwelcome debt.

Earlier the king dumped a whole huge pile of money on him and Joe got into financial debt. Then the King dumped a whole huge pile of mercy on him ... and if he receives it, he's in debt to the King's mercy. He knows that if he's really grateful - if he takes this mercy into his heart - then he's actually exchanging one un-payable debt for another.

You think he wants to be grateful for the rest of his life? No way! He could never pay it back. He'd never get even. So he didn't take the mercy into his heart. He took the mercy into his hand and used it for what he could get out of it. Then he threw it away He didn't have any left when he got to me.

King:

So now he's in prison. Well, he chose it. That isn't what I want for him. My heart is as full of mercy for him now as it was then. But how can I give him a gift if he doesn't want it, and won't take it?

Witness: That *is* me!

Jackie's story: "Beloved"

When I was in playschool I got yelled at for spilling ice cream on my dress and shamed in front of my classmates. I was so afraid to say anything to the teacher that day that I wouldn't even ask to go to the toilet. When I got home I rushed to the toilet and had an accident on the way and was punished for that as well. That's my earliest memory of when I began to "wear" shame. A lot of things I did over the years caused shame to grow in me. And it became the banner that I lived under for years.

When I was going into primary school my parents got divorced. It uprooted much of my security and I began living with fear. I would always begin sentences with "I'm afraid to ..."" I didn't recognize that I was doing this until I was 25.

In the middle school and High school years when "looks" are everything, I'd look in the mirror and be disgusted with what I saw. My little sister was always the beautiful one and when I compared myself to her, I'd say to myself "you're a fat ugly slob". But it wasn't just my appearance: I was unacceptable.

When I first met Jesus it seemed as if my whole life changed. After asking him to come into my life, I experienced a flood of his love in me. And, for a while, it seemed like life would be just perfect from that point on. That was such a wonderful time for me. I was aware that God was not far off and distant but that he was always with me. He even knew everything I was thinking and feeling. But, although I had a very real and powerful experience of meeting Jesus, there

172

were still parts of my heart that had not yet received him as Saviour; places that did not know his love, his grace or his mercy. I was in bondage to things I didn't even know were there.

One day I sat down and watched a film. During the film there was a scene where the name of Jesus was cursed. This came as a big shock to me. A battle began in my thought life. My mind started to become flooded with all sorts of foul words against God and all things holy. It became worse when I'd go to communion. I was scared to death. As shame and fear grew, the thoughts got worse. I didn't think I could talk to God about this, so I tried to make the thoughts stop on my own. But I couldn't.

One night my husband and I were with some friends. One of the men started talking about blaspheming against the Holy Spirit. He said that if someone did that they would die and never be forgiven. I thought, "I have blasphemed the Holy Spirit in my thought life and if I die tonight, I'm going to go to hell."

With that thought, I felt as if a truckload of fear was dumped into my stomach and I was covered in complete darkness. I began to shake and my husband tried to hold me and console me but I couldn't stop shaking. I was so afraid that I was going to die. I kept all the lights on in the house and I didn't sleep at all that night. I kept praying for God to forgive me and begging him not to leave me.

Early that morning I began reading the Bible, trying to fill my mind with what was pure and continually asking God to forgive me, pleading with him to help me get rid of these thoughts.

This became an everyday struggle for me. So, in order to counter the thoughts I was having, I would constantly be moving my mouth, speaking good things to God so that he'd know that what was coming from my mouth was what was really in my heart. It seemed like I was going crazy but the constant moving of my lips was what kept me from falling over the edge.

As time went on I thought - "I guess this is how I'm going to be living the rest of my life. I'm going to be struggling with this until I die." My constant prayer was, "God please don't leave me". I did seek help from my pastor at the time and from others. My pastor said that if I was worried then I hadn't lost my salvation. I was told by well meaning friends that I just needed to trust God. Nothing helped. I didn't trust God. I feared him. Even though I had had a very real experience of God's presence, I didn't really know my heavenly Father.

I began to rationalize that if I couldn't please God with my thoughts, I could try to figure out what he wanted me to do and then do it perfectly so that he would accept me. I followed a strict list of rules that I made up for myself. I believed that if I didn't do what I thought God wanted me to do or if I did it imperfectly then he'd be angry with me and want nothing more to do with me. The God I believed in was the God with the perpetually knitted eyebrows, ready to punish me at the slightest failure.

I would put my every action under a microscope and scrutinize my every move, pointing out to myself where I had failed and hating myself for those failures. I would cry by my children when they were asleep and beg God to change me so I wouldn't ruin them.. I couldn't live up to my own expectations. I lived in self-judgement.

The way out

Reflection: "That's just like my Father"

In the parable of the "Unmerciful Servant", Jesus tells of a king who pours out a great shower of mercy upon his servant. This mercy was a gift of grace: the servant was given mercy instead of what he had earned and what he deserved.

This is the way it is with our Father. But as important as this truth is to all who know the Father's mercy, it can be just a bit comfortable for us. It is less comfortable for us to recognize that this gift comes with "strings attached". If the servant receives this gift, he is, as the fellow servant says in the reflection above, simply "exchanging one unpayable debt for another". Surely Jesus is making this very point in his description of the king's response to the merciless behaviour of his servant: *"You wicked servant ... I cancelled all that debt of yours because you begged me to. Shouldn't you have had mercy on your fellow servant just as I had on you?"* This is a rhetorical question. The Greek word translated here as "shouldn't" is "dei" which means "... an unavoidable, urgent, compulsory necessity". And this is a necessity that attaches to something "by the nature of things".

This means that the servant didn't leave out something optional; he failed to do what was absolutely necessary. The nature of God's mercy is such that if one receives it as a gift one must turn and give it away. So the gift of mercy is not like the gift of a bicycle. If I receive a bicycle as a gift there is nothing about the nature of that bike which, in itself, means I must now turn and give it away. Quite the opposite: the bicycle is mine. I can take it in my hands and use it as I wish; I can ride it or throw it away. I can receive it and actually "have it" with or without genuine thanksgiving or gratitude or any change of heart. Gratitude would be nice when such a gift is given - it might even be expected - but it's not necessary. I retain the bike even if the giver walks away muttering that I am ungrateful.

Not so with mercy. The lack of a merciful response in the heart and in the life of one who has received God's mercy is so at odds with the very nature of mercy itself that one can say the lack indicates that the gift has not actually been received at all. If I receive it and "have" it, I *will* give it. *It is literally impossible for me to "have mercy" without giving it.* This is true of all the things of the kingdom of God. For example, I cannot "have" the Father's love, nor his life without giving those away [*consider* 1 John 4:19-21]. If I try to "preserve" them or keep them for myself, I lose them. On the other hand, the more we give away (*invest*), the more we have.

So it is with forgiveness, which is the form of mercy Jesus is addressing in this parable. If we are forgiven but do not forgive "this is how [our] heavenly Father will treat each of [us]": we will get what we have earned and what we deserve [vs.34-35]! This, friends, is a frightening prospect! But what else can we expect? After all, if we reject the nature of the gift by refusing to give it away, we reject the gift itself ... and the giver.

So the deeper truth about mercy is that it is not something that I "have" in any conventional sense at all. "It" only exists as a way of being - as an outward expression of the attitude and disposition of my heart. This is because mercy is not a commodity I possess - or that God "possesses" for that matter - rather mercy is part of the nature of the God who gives himself to me. The gift of his mercy is a gift of himself.

When I realize that this gift of mercy is essential to life for me, how can I receive that life - or, better yet, how can I receive him as he is coming *as* life for me - without surrendering my life to the Lord who *is* mercy? Because of the nature of the gift and the giver, I must respond by living in debt, as one who can never repay the giver; as one who can never "get even" and whose joy it is to live the Father's merciful life in gratitude. As I live this life, a wonderful way opens up: both the nature of his mercy *and his merciful nature* can now be expressed in and through me. To receive him is to become like him. To receive mercy is to become merciful.

But there is more: to receive mercy is to receive *power*. Mercy is the power we are given to destroy the works of judgement [James 2:13].

Last but not least, mercy is a fundamental sign of God's life in us. So says the apostle Peter when he names and celebrates the transforming grace of the Father who calls us out of the darkness of idolatry into the light of his life. He speaks of the grace which makes of us a "royal priesthood". The shared, unifying experience of this grace is the hallmark and the festal shout of the chosen people of God: *"We have received mercy!"* [1 Peter 2:9-10]

Witness: That *is* my Father! Witness of truth spoken in love.

Jackie's Story: Beloved, Part II

Because I thought I was not lovable, I was always looking for evidence as to why that was the case. And when you're looking for evidence you'll find it: I found plenty wrong with me. Eventually I went to another pastor for counselling. There I received some wonderful inner healing.

I shared with him that others thought I was always too hard on myself. My pastor said, "In some respects you may be hard on yourself but in another, you are not hard enough on yourself." Then he read the parable of the "unmerciful servant" from the Gospel of Matthew. My Pastor said "Just as that servant was unmerciful toward his friend, you are being unmerciful with yourself, you are standing in constant judgement over and condemnation of yourself."

As we began to pray, God showed me a picture of myself at 17. I saw what I had been doing to myself all these years and it broke my heart. I saw how I had despised this girl. I never had any use for her unless she was perfect. I saw all the damage that I caused by constantly judging and condemning myself. Then God showed me his love and compassion for me in the midst of my judgement. I asked him to forgive me for judging myself. There are times when we ask God to forgive us but we are unable to forgive ourselves. I had to make a conscious choice to open my hands to receive God's mercy and forgiveness and then turn and offer it to myself.

This was a giant step forward towards a new way of being with myself. But I needed to practice living in mercy. I needed a lot of practice. Sometimes I'd fall hard. I'd have a hard day and yell at my husband and the kids. Then I'd be upset with myself for that so I'd go to the freezer and pull out some ice cream and finish it off. Then I'd be even more disgusted with myself and I'd spiral down into the abyss of self condemnation. But Jesus would meet me there and remind me of the way out: mercy.

One of the ways I needed to practice living in mercy was to stop calling myself names like, "stupid idiot." That took a lot of work. And there was more: I asked Jesus to reveal my heart to me; I asked him to give me his eyes for me; I gave him all the stuff that was in my heart like anger, fear, pride and bitterness, then I asked him to give me what was in his heart: his Truth, his Love, his Life.

I desperately needed to know God as the God of mercy. I needed to really know him and to learn to hear his voice. Until I could hear his voice in my life, I was stuck with my own! Because I struggled so much with my thoughts, I was sure God couldn't speak to me or wouldn't. Then one day he did.

I was driving on the highway and I had a thought that came very strongly to me. I felt that I ought to stop for the next car I saw on the side of the highway. I said, "Is that you God? All right. If there is a car, I'll stop." A little way down the highway I saw a car and my heart dropped into my stomach. "Oh no! Now I have to stop! Oh Lord, I hope it's a *woman! Please God, let it be a woman!" So I parked far away from the car. As I got out, praying the whole time, a woman came out of the other car and shouted, "Thank you Jesus!! Someone finally stopped!" I was thinking, "Thank you Jesus! It's a woman and I'm safe!"*

I did the best I could to help her and went home so excited thinking, "Wow, God actually spoke to me." But it was more than that. I came to understand that it wasn't so much that he wanted me to do something for him - he was letting me know that he loved me and that he hadn't left me. And I really needed to know that He loved me. It would take the next several years for me to begin to believe and trust in that love because I didn't love myself.

God began to teach me about who he is through the births of my children:

My first daughter was born 3 months premature and weighed 2½ lbs. The whole ordeal was very intense but in the midst of it all I felt God's grace sustaining me. I knew he was with us and caring for us.

While pregnant with my son, my greatest prayer was, "God please don't let this baby weigh 8 lbs or over. I just had a tiny 2 pounder and I don't think I can handle giving birth to a huge baby. The day he was born he weighed in at 7 lbs 15oz. I giggled and thought "Lord you are so funny". And you know what? His eyebrows began to relax.

My third child was going to be a boy. I was sure God told me this child would be a boy and I had the scripture verse he gave me to back it up. When this child was born, the doctor announced that it was a girl. It was such a wonderful surprise and I cried for joy because of God's goodness.

Through my first child he showed me that he is the God who is with me, the God who cares for me. With my second, he showed me that he is the God who makes me laugh. And with my third, he showed me that he is the God who surprises me. In all of it, he showed me how much he loves me.

"Wow, God loves ME. He really loves me." As I began to really believe that, my relationship with him began to deepen and grow. I could begin to trust that he would not leave me or hate me. I began to trust him even with my horrible thought life. I began to really believe that I was God's child. I could stand in the truth that he gave me about who I am and I began to notice that I was getting free of the fear and horrible thoughts I had.

With all the wonderful healing I had received, my devotional life was getting better. My time with the Lord used to be a very anxious time for me. I would sit down with my bible open and try to figure out all the things I was doing wrong. And then I would write a list of what I needed to do to change. I'd follow it for a few days but it didn't last long. So I always saw God as angry and disappointed with me. But now that he had done so much healing in me, my devotional time began to change. Jesus would say "Just be with me". I would ask him, "How do I just be with you?"

I'd read in the psalm about "delighting myself in the Lord". I wanted to, but I didn't know how.

One day I was taking a shower and a picture flashed in my mind. It was of my wedding day. And I saw my husband's face and he looked really happy. I thought, "Wow, my husband was actually happy to be married to me!" I had such a sense of shame for so long that I could never accept that someone could actually enjoy me for me. I came out of the shower and I shared with my husband what I saw. I said "Darling, you were actually happy to be married to me!" " Well dear, of course I was happy!"

This picture that God gave me deepened my relationship with my husband but was also giving me a picture of God's love for me. I could actually imagine the possibility of delighting myself in my heavenly Father.

And then a new concept came to me: God takes delight in me! I could never entertain that possibility before, but now I was receiving a new truth. GOD DELIGHTS IN ME. He actually enjoys me and I can enjoy him. I can live from his mercy. I can love myself and I can begin to love others as he loves them. And for the first time I could see that I was actually growing.

One of the best things I learned to do was to ask Jesus to reveal my heart to me. It doesn't always feel like the best thing at the time because of the stuff he shows me like judgement, anger, and pride. But now I can receive the truth: I don't need to be the judge over my own life. I can entrust that to him.

Apart from God, I have no mercy for myself or others. He continually offers me his mercy and love and invites me into a deeper relationship with him.

One night he gave me a formal invitation. I opened my bible to Song of Songs and as I read, I wrote in my journal: "Then the one who loves my soul spoke to me and said, 'Arise my darling, my beautiful one, and come with me (come be with me). See the winter is past; the rains are over and gone. Flowers appear on the earth, the season of singing has come...show me your face, let me hear your voice; for your voice is sweet and your face is lovely ...'" New life was beginning in my time with the Lord. I could come and sit with him and know that he wanted me there - I could delight myself in him and not be afraid.

As I look back, I realize that God was not going to take away my problems or change my circumstances. He was going to come to me right where I was in my weakness and deepest despair. He came to free me from judgement and bring me into his mercy. He was giving me a new heart: one that would become more like Jesus' heart.

The truth is he isn't done with me yet. I still call myself names every now and then. But now when something is stirring in me, something ugly, or when I'm filled with anxiety, I know that I get to start over again. Instead of spiralling downward into despair, I flee to his heart of mercy. And there he reminds me of my new name: "Beloved.

Path Out of the Courtroom: with Jesus, looking at our hearts; receiving and responding to the Father's love expressed in truth.

Questions: Do you believe that you have, at least at times, been an unmerciful servant in the relationship you have with yourself? Have you called yourself names? Have you turned from the mercy of God, gripped yourself by the throat and demanded that you pay all that you owe?

Love in Truth: Mercy is never something that can be earned or deserved. That fact means that if you receive the mercy Jesus has for you, you will be in debt - a debt that can never be repaid. Jesus died for you so that you may live joyfully in debt to the mercy of God. If you have, at least in part, taken the Father's mercy into your hands only, it is time to open your hands and release the Father's mercy into your heart. It is time to receive the grace to become a merciful servant:

Prayer Path:

Prayer of the Merciful Servant

Jesus, I know that you are making it possible for me to love myself as you love me. I thank you for your mercy, your forgiveness, your _____, and I choose, in the power of your love, to withhold nothing of you from myself: I receive your mercy; I receive your forgiveness; I receive your _____. I want to be like you, Jesus. I want to be filled with mercy. In your presence I now open my hands and I release your mercy, and all your gracious gifts, into my mind and heart so that I can grow into the abundant life you intend for me. Thank you, Jesus.

The Way In

Reflection: The Parable Turned Inside Out

What would things look like if we were merciful servants? We could, of course, turn the parable of the unmerciful servant "inside out" by changing the way the servant responds in the parable: he turns to his fellow servant with the mercy he has truly received and forgives that small debt. But another way is available. In Luke's gospel there is a picture given to us of a man to whom Jesus extends extravagant mercy and who, unlike the king's servant, turns and joyfully makes the kind of offering that can only come from a heart where mercy has actually been received. This man is not a character in a parable but a real man who had a real encounter with Jesus one particular day as the Lord was passing through Jericho on his way to the cross...

A tax collector gets in debt

Jesus entered Jericho and was passing through. A man was there by the name of Zacchaeus; he was a chief tax collector and was wealthy. He wanted to see who Jesus was, but being a short man he could not, because of the crowd. So he ran ahead and climbed a sycamore-fig tree to see him, since Jesus was coming that way. When Jesus reached the spot, he looked up and said to him, "Zacchaeus, come down immediately. I must stay at your house today." So he came down at once and welcomed him gladly. All the people saw this and began to mutter, "He has gone to be the guest of a 'sinner.' " But Zacchaeus stood up and said to the Lord, "Look, Lord! Here and now I give half of my possessions to the poor, and if I have cheated anybody out of anything, I will pay back four times the amount." Jesus said to him, "Today salvation has come to this house, because this man, too, is a son of Abraham. For the Son of Man came to seek and to save what was lost." [Luke 19:1-10]

This man - this tax collector - serves Rome, the power which occupies Palestine and oppresses his people. Zacchaeus is considered a traitor by the Jews, classed with criminals, universally despised and prohibited from entering the synagogue. His riches cannot purchase a place for him among his people as a "son of Abraham". In their eyes he has forfeited any claim to be a "son". He is nothing but a "sinner".

Jesus singles him out and calls him by name. Unthinkable. He expresses a desire to be with Zacchaeus. Outrageous. He comes into the sinner's house and enters into table fellowship with him. Defiling. Scandalous.

And Zacchaeus? The Lord's mercy is not wasted on him. His response to Jesus is a joyful song of thanksgiving. Every aspect of his response shouts "I have received mercy!" He turns immediately with a new heart and extends the mercy he has received. First, his mercy goes out to the poor: his giving is so sacrificial and extravagant that one may assume his external life will never be the same again. This is fitting: his internal life will never be the same again. Then Zacchaeus goes well beyond anything required in law as he seeks to make restitution for wrong he has done. He is not trying to earn something. He is giving away the precious gift he could not earn.

Mercy has overcome judgement there in the life of Zacchaeus. The power of the pointed finger has been overturned by the power of the familial embrace of his Saviour and Lord and only

Judge. Zacchaeus is filled with joy because he knows it's true: he is a son again! And glad to be in debt.

Witness: Just like him. Where we're going: witness of the Father's children

The Widow of Danbury

This widow's husband had died at age 37 in the middle of the cold winter of 1953, leaving her with three children to care for. She was filled with grief - lost in a very deep and dark place. She cried out to God, pleading with him to lift her out of the depths she was in so that she could be with him. And God spoke to her. He gave her to know that he was there with her in the depths. She didn't have to do anything or go anywhere, because her Saviour had come to the place where she was. She had been found.

A few months after her husband's death, the widow of Danbury had a dream on Easter night. This was a dream too real to be called a dream. It was as real as anything she had ever experienced, waking or sleeping. It was a vision. In her vision she saw Jesus coming toward her and her husband was with him. All of the pain and grief of her loss was reversed in an instant; she felt a surge of unspeakable joy because she knew that her husband was being restored to her. She began to run toward him. But before she reached him she was overcome with thanksgiving - with a profound sense of gratitude. Right then she stopped, knelt down and gave thanks to God for bringing her husband back to her.

When she looked up again, Jesus and her husband were gone, and for a second time she experienced the full impact of suddenly losing the man she loved. This grief was no less devastating than the first, and it contained another bitterly painful ingredient: the thought that if she just hadn't stopped to give thanks, she would have reached him and known what is was to hold her husband in her arms again.

A short time later, through prayer with a friend, Jesus began to heal her. Eventually she understood the purpose of her vision. A deep assurance began to grow up in her: she knew in her heart that her husband was with Jesus. She was filled with gratitude again.

The Widow of Danbury. Althea Benedict, was my mother. She managed to keep her family together, but she never earned enough to, as she said, "have the privilege of paying taxes." An unexpected expense of as little as five or ten dollars could wreck the budget for the month. She had been left with no financial security and it disturbed her to think that if she were to die, her children would be left with nothing. She had no life insurance.

Then one day an incredible and utterly unexpected thing happened: she came into possession, through an anonymous gift in the mail, of what seemed like a small fortune to her: sixty five dollars! She knew exactly what she wanted to do with it: this money would go for insurance.

But the Lord spoke to her and said that she was to give the money away to someone who really needed it. He said she was to trust him and that he would care for her children. Immediately she went to her minister, gave him the money and told him to use it as he saw fit to help someone in need.

We know, as I am sure my mother knew, that there were many good reasons for keeping the money. Who wouldn't have praised her for giving any portion of it away - perhaps a tithe - considering her circumstances. But she gave all of it away. I believe she was obedient because she was thankful. She was thankful because the Lord had been there with her in the depths. He had assured her of his eternal love for her husband, and she knew that her Saviour could be trusted to care for her children.

Radical reliance upon God is not common. In the wisdom of the world such trust is at least foolish. But trust is built on a firm foundation: trust is the capacity of one who has a thankful heart. Our hearts are made thankful when we receive the one who has come and loved us right where we are; the one who gives himself to us. To receive that grace is to be in debt and to know the joy of giving the gift we have received.

Path of the Father's Child. Freedom in the One who is truth: who we are; who he is; affirming the truth in prayer.

Questions: Is the Lord asking you to give away the gifts that he has given you? What place does gratitude have in your heart? Can you

189

be grateful to God without trusting him? Can you trust him without being grateful to him? Do you desire to be in debt to the mercy of God?

Love in Truth: You can measure the extent to which you have received God's mercy by the measure of the genuine mercy you extend to yourself and others (not to be confused with the *verdict* of "innocent"!). Mercy can only be received at the feet of the Righteous Judge as he sits on the throne of your life.

Prayer Path of the Father's Child. Praying the truth: who he is and who we are

Prayer at the feet of the Judge

Jesus, I want you to be the only judge of my life. I want to sit at your feet.

Jesus, I want to be more grateful to you, to trust you more and to be in greater debt to your mercy.

Holy Spirit, fill me with the grace to live from you and be led by you. Holy Spirit, give me the power to become the person I was created to be. Help me to be my Father's child.

Father, I want to know you as my Abba.
Father, please tell me who I am, every day.

Holy Trinity - Father, Son and Holy Spirit:
      I surrender my life to you.
      I surrender my will to you.

I surrender my judgement, my ways, my desires and my plans to you.

Holy Trinity - Father, Son and Holy Spirit:

I want to:

be in your will,

receive your mercy,

walk in your way,

love what you love,

hate what you hate,

follow your plan for me,

live your life.

In the Name of God: Father, Son and Holy Spirit

✝

The Father's love for two sons
Grace to enter in

The Parable
Luke 15:11-32

[11]*Jesus continued: "There was a man who had two sons.* [12]*The younger one said to his father, 'Father, give me my share of the estate.' So he divided his property between them.*

[13]*"Not long after that, the younger son got together all he had, set off for a distant country and there squandered his wealth in wild living.* [14]*After he had spent everything, there was a severe famine in that whole country, and he began to be in need.* [15]*So he went and hired himself out to a citizen of that country, who sent him to his fields to feed pigs.* [16]*He longed to fill his stomach with the pods that the pigs were eating, but no one gave him anything.*

[17]*"When he came to his senses, he said, 'How many of my father's hired men have food to spare, and here I am starving to death!* [18]*I will set out and go back to my father and say to him: Father, I have sinned against heaven and against you.* [19]*I am no longer worthy to be called your son; make me like one of your hired men.'* [20]*So he got up and went to his father.*

"But while he was still a long way off, his father saw him and was filled with compassion for him; he ran to his son, threw his arms around him and kissed him.

²¹ "The son said to him, 'Father, I have sinned against heaven and against you. I am no longer worthy to be called your son.'

²² "But the father said to his servants, 'Quick! Bring the best robe and put it on him. Put a ring on his finger and sandals on his feet. ²³Bring the fattened calf and kill it. Let's have a feast and celebrate. ²⁴For this son of mine was dead and is alive again; he was lost and is found.' So they began to celebrate.

²⁵ "Meanwhile, the older son was in the field. When he came near the house, he heard music and dancing. ²⁶So he called one of the servants and asked him what was going on. ²⁷ 'Your brother has come,' he replied, 'and your father has killed the fattened calf because he has him back safe and sound.'

²⁸ "The older brother became angry and refused to go in. So his father went out and pleaded with him. ²⁹But he answered his father, 'Look! All these years I've been slaving for you and never disobeyed your orders. Yet you never gave me even a young goat so I could celebrate with my friends. ³⁰But when this son of yours who has squandered your property with prostitutes comes home, you kill the fattened calf for him!'

³¹ " 'My son,' the father said, 'you are always with me, and everything I have is yours. ²But we had to celebrate and be glad, because this brother of yours was dead and is alive again; he was lost and is found.'"

Reflection: "That's just like me"

This is the Father all of us should have had and some of us wish we had been. We were made for the unconditional love that fills the heart of this father. The full rivers of grace flowing within the relationships in this parable stream entirely from his direction. The father is the source of all mercy, all compassion, all grace. What do the sons contribute? Mostly a kind of pollution: callous disregard, self-serving calculation, rejection, self-absorption and bitter judgement.

The younger son comes to his father to ask for an inheritance that, although it could come to him any time his father should decide to "retire" from managing his estate, would normally come to a son only with his father's death. Given that, what does his request amount to? Anything from "Could you pretend that your active life of authority is over so that I can take what's mine and leave?" to "Father, if you would just become as though you were dead for me, I could really start living!" The younger son then manages to sink further down from this low start. He goes on to waste this provision - the fruit of his father's life - on a journey that goes from palatial dissipation to pigpen realization. Starving, he comes to his senses in the company of unclean pigs, remembering that even his father's hired servants have enough to eat. They are not members of the family, but it may have occurred to this young man that if he gets what's coming to him, he will no longer be considered a member of the family either, much less a son, after what he has done. He conceives a plan to secure for himself the best he can hope for. He memorizes his speech. He heads home.

Meanwhile the older son abides in the field, watching over his hired hands by day. Then he hears news of his brother's appearing and of his reception - as though he is a shining gift straight from heaven. The reaction of the older brother to the news of a party going on, and to the pleas of his father to come in and join the celebration, are a window into his heart. Though he is a son, he views himself as a slave and carries a slave's resentment [vs. 29a]. He is offended by the party. His response might remind us of Jonah's response to the mercy of God given to the people of Nineveh [Jonah 4]: "I just knew it! I knew you were too merciful and loving and compassionate to follow through. I knew they'd get off. They sinned all day, only repenting at the last minute, and what did they get? They got a big, fat party! I did what was right, prophesying all day, and what did I get? I got to look like a fool. Oh, and your prophet got no shade whatsoever. Zero."

Jonah didn't stop with delivering the Lord's judgement, he entered into his own. As a result he could not enter into the Lord's mercy for Nineveh. So it is with the older son: he can't enter the house where mercy is lived and celebrated: he resents mercy, as Jonah did, as a miscarriage of justice. He has judged himself, his brother and his father. Filled with judgement, he spews out all the evidence he has collected to support the cases he has made and the verdicts he has handed down.

If this son could only see the condition of his heart and be open to see his father's heart! If he only knew his true and desperate condition: he has turned from the joy it is to be his father's son and is dead to the abundant life given to him. This beloved son is lost and in bondage to bitterness. If the older son were to "come to his senses" he would go to his father and he would say "Father, I have sinned against heaven and against you. I am no longer worthy to be called your son." This would not be a ploy. He would go to his father filled, not with judgement, but with deep sorrow and it's fruit: true repentance. He would go in tears: "Have mercy, Father! Please forgive me!" He would receive all his Father has for him: not rewards to be claimed based upon worthiness, but as free gifts of his father's love. He would come in and know joy with his brother in their father's house.

Witness: That *is* me!

In "The Hiding Place" Corrie ten Boom tells of the tortured days she endured with her sister, Betsie, at Vught, a German concentration camp for political prisoners in Holland. They had been arrested, along with their mother and father and others in the family, for taking Jews into their home and helping them to escape Nazi persecution. Their arrest came about through betrayal by a fellow countryman. A deep and bitter judgement concerning that betrayal rose up to poison Corrie when, after working separate jobs in the prison one day, she and Betsie exchanged news. Betsie had discovered the name of their betrayer:

Corrie in the Courtroom

... *"A lady from Ermelo was transferred to the sewing detail today. When I introduced myself, she said, 'Another one!'"*

"What did she mean?"

"Corrie, do you remember, the day we were arrested, a man came to the shop? You were sick and I had to wake you up."

I remembered very well. Remembered the strange roving eyes, the uneasiness in the pit of my stomach that was more than fever.

"Apparently everyone in Ermelo knew him. He worked with the Gestapo from the first day of occupation. He reported this woman's two brothers for Resistance work, and finally herself and her

husband too" When Ermelo had finally caught on to him he had come to Harlem and teamed up with Willemse and Kapteyn. His name was Jan Vogel.

Flames of fire seemed to leap around that name in my heart. I thought of father's final hours, alone and confused, in a hospital corridor. Of the underground work so abruptly halted. I thought of Mary Itallie arrested while walking down a street. And I knew that if Jan Vogel stood in front of me now I could kill him.

Betsie drew the little cloth bag from beneath her overalls and held it out to me, but I shook my head. Betsie kept the Bible during the day, since she had more chance to read and teach from it here than I did at the Phillips barracks. In the evenings we held a clandestine prayer meeting for as many as could crowd around our bunk.

"You lead the prayers tonight, Betsie. I have a headache."

More than a headache. All of me ached with the violence of my feelings about the man who had done us so much harm. That night I did not sleep and the next day at my bench scarcely heard the conversation around me. By the end of the week I had worked myself into such a sickness of body and spirit that Mr Moorman stopped at my bench to ask if something were wrong.

"Wrong? Yes, something's wrong!" And I plunged into an account of that morning. I was only too eager to tell Mr Moorman and all Holland how Jan Vogel had betrayed his country.

The way out

Reflection: "That's just like my Father"

The parable about a loving father and his two sons found in the fifteenth chapter of Luke is commonly called the parable of "The Prodigal Son". But if it were primarily about sons it would be about two sons, not just the younger wasteful one. Surely it would be about the older wasteful one as well. But it is not essentially about sons at all: this parable is a revelation Jesus gives us about his Father. We can hardly believe it, but it is true: this is who our God and Father is - the truth about his heart for us. This truth meets us in the place where we live in fear - *not* "holy fear" - and where we do *not* know his perfect love [1 John 4:18]. It comes into our broken, judging hearts with the wonderful truth that the Father's ways are not our ways nor his thoughts our thoughts.

Some years ago the Father spoke these words into my heart: "I am not counting your sins. I am measuring the distance." I reflect on those words in my book "*Not As Orphans*" as follows:

> *"I am measuring the distance." Not the distance between me and the person I ought to be. Not the distance I need to go to measure up. What my Father measures is the distance between us...*
>
> *We can know something of this. For instance, if we have suffered estrangement from a child - if we have seen our child going destructive ways and known the agony of a gulf widening between us. In the midst of this kind of loss, what do we measure? Do we keep track of her sins for a future reckoning? Or does our heart measure the distance and long for her return? When he comes near again do we point the finger, or*

do we reach out with open hands to draw him into our arms?

My Father measures the distance. When I return to him and he embraces me, I know that he has not been counting my sins. I feel the joy of his measuring heart."

This was spoken directly to me - it didn't come through reading this parable, but it could have. The Father who spoke to me was the Father Jesus reveals - the one who searches the horizon watching for our return; who rejoices over the found coin, the found sheep and the found son [Luke 15:1-10]. Jesus is the Word about this Father who *is* mercy and who opens up a perfect way for both younger and older sons to know the extent of that mercy. The Father's mercy is the door "sons" go through in order to come in and rejoice in their Father's house. The fact that this abundant mercy was rejected by the older son does not change his father's heart. *He loves both sons extravagantly before, during and after anything they do.*

It is important to consider the context for this parable: Jesus is meeting with and teaching tax collectors and "sinners". The Pharisees and the teachers of the law observe him and mutter, "This man welcomes sinners and eats with them." This sounds just like the "older brother"! They are so like him. They have tried to serve their Father without loving as he loves. They look at their brothers and see only "sinners". They judge themselves as innocent. They are offended by and resent the attentions given to those who they believe have disqualified themselves from association with the righteous - in this case, the merciful, gracious attentions shown by a man who speaks with a power and authority unprecedented and undeniable; who cannot simply be dismissed; who eats with the "righteous" but who holds up a mirror to their hypocrisy [ex Luke 14:1-14; 16:14-15]. The resentful older son accumulated evidence against his father and his brother with which he angrily confronts his father. These Pharisees and teachers are walking the same path: they are looking for evidence in the "case" they are building against Jesus [15:1].

When Jesus speaks about the older brother is he speaking about them? I believe he is; but not just *about* them. If the Pharisees and the teachers of the law are represented in the bitterly judging older son, then the father's words spoken to him are spoken, not just *about* them, but *to* them: "My son...you are always with me, and everything I have is yours." Consider this: Jesus responds to those who resent, judge and plot against him with a story that reveals their hard hearts but which also reveals that the Father's heart is filled with mercy and love for them. Through this parable coming in this context Jesus is personally demonstrating the same love that is the subject of the parable itself.

In Jesus, the Father's merciful love was available to Pharisees then and to us now. These words are spoken to real and lost sons by the Father of the Saviour of all "sinners" and all those who are "righteous". These are words of life for sons and daughters, old and young, then and now. And what gracious, heartbreakingly merciful words they are: "My son ... you are always with me, and everything I have is yours." "Come in!" he is saying; "Be glad! Celebrate!" And his eyes assure us that he will be there celebrating with us ... and not reluctantly.

There is only one way in to the Father's house. All must enter through the door of mercy. All enter that door by means of repentance and reconciliation. Only "sons" enter. The robe, the ring and the sonship shoes are pure gifts of the Father's love. All were dead but are alive again. All were lost but are found.

Witness: That *is* my Father! Witness of truth spoken in love.

Corrie in the Courtroom, Part II

What puzzled me all this time was Betsie. She had suffered everything I had and yet she seemed to carry no burden of rage. "Betsie!" I hissed one dark night when I knew that my restless tossing must be keeping her awake. Three of us now shared this single cot as the crowded camp daily received new arrivals. "Betsie, don't you feel anything about Jan Vogel? Doesn't it bother you?"

"Oh yes, Corrie! Terribly! I've felt for him ever since I knew - and pray for him whenever his name comes into my mind. How dreadfully he must be suffering!"

For a long time I lay silent in the huge shadowy barracks restless with the sighs, snores, and stirrings of hundreds of women. Once again I had the feeling that this sister with whom I had spent all my life belonged somehow to another order of beings. Wasn't she telling me in her gentle way that I was as guilty as Jan Vogel? Didn't he and I stand together before an all-seeing God convicted of the same sin of murder? For I had murdered him with my heart and with my tongue.

"Lord Jesus," I whispered into the lumpy ticking of the bed, "I forgive Jan Vogel as I pray that you will forgive me. I have done him great damage. Bless him now, and his family ..." That night for the first time since our betrayer had a name I slept deep

and dreamlessly until the whistle summoned us to roll call.

Path Out of the Courtroom: with Jesus, looking at our hearts; receiving and responding to the Father's love expressed in truth.

Questions: Is your path more like that of the younger or of the older brother? If you are more like the younger brother, have you actually allowed yourself to enter and celebrate as a "son"? Has an awareness of the depth of your sin shown you the depth of his mercy and love? If you are more like the older brother, what might it mean for you to "come to your senses"? What would you think? What would you feel? What would you do?

As you digest this parable are you prepared to shift your focus from what you think and feel about yourself to what your heavenly Father thinks and feels about you?

Love in Truth: Our identity is given to us as a gift of the Father's love. If the Father tells us who we are to him, then we know who we are. There is nothing more to be said: the Father wants to tell you who you are. It is time to listen.

Prayer Path: The following words were spoken by the Father in power deep into the heart of a dear brother in the Maranatha Community in the UK. They were given very personally for him. But they were also given to lift me and you higher up into the life of freedom in Christ Jesus - the life which is the gift of grace and truth. As you read this living word, anointed by the Holy Spirit for you, listen to your Abba. He will tell you the truth of who you are to him. That and nothing else *is* who you are. Listen every day.

Abba's word to Juan - and to us

You are dearly loved

You are intimately known

You are valued beyond price

You are precious

The Way In

Reflection: The Parable Turned Inside Out

There was a father who had two teenage sons. The older son was seventeen. The younger son, who had been adopted when he was twelve, was now fifteen. One day the father was sitting on the couch in his living room reading the paper. He caught a glimpse of something out of the corner of his eye and looked up. From where he was sitting he could see beyond the living room, through a narrow hall into the kitchen. He had an unobstructed view of his younger, adopted son approaching the refrigerator, obviously unaware that his father was watching him. The young man paused at the refrigerator door, took hold of the handle, looked to his left, then back, then opened the door about half way. He peered around the door at the things on the shelves there, then, after a very brief peek into the stuffed caverns of the interior, he took hold of something up front on the middle shelf. Propping the door with one foot he went quickly to work with both hands. After no more than 10 seconds he let the door slowly shut as he walked quietly away with what looked like one small pickle.

"He wasn't quite furtive" thought his father, "but it wasn't far from it. He just looked uncomfortable; like he wasn't sure it was all right for him to be there; like it's not really his refrigerator. True: it's my refrigerator, but what's mine is his. Maybe I'll go find him in a minute and ask him if just that one stunted pickle did it for him... maybe sound him out a little. I love that boy. But sometimes I wonder if he knows it ... I wonder if he knows who he is."

Well before the "minute" was up, the father saw his older son enter the kitchen. He watched him take hold of the handle and more or less fling the refrigerator door all the gaping wide way open; watched him take up a stance in front that looked remarkably like one hip was out of joint. Then, with his hands laced on his head, he began his inspection. He stared for a few seconds, then lifted a huge bottle of orange juice from the refrigerator door and unscrewed the lid. Looking on from behind, his father saw the bottle tilt up above his son's head - heard rivers go glugging down. Then his son lowered the bottle, put it on the counter still open and wiped his lips with his sleeve. "Ahhhhh", he said. "Just keeping his strength up 'til he finds something" his father thought.

Then the young man got to work. He began to move things around, picking items up, rejecting some, choosing others for the growing jumble on the counter. He worked every shelf. Finally he slowed down and just as he began to gather things together, an amazing thing happened. His father became aware of a kind of rippling sensation starting way down deep in the pit of his stomach. In a split second he knew for certain that the ripple was laughter forming - that there was no keeping this down and that he had no desire whatsoever to resist. Within a few seconds he could feel the laughter rising up through him, growing and growing as it came, until it burst out loud. He threw his head back. He laughed from the bottom up. He laughed from the top down. His son turned, his eyes wide. He began to grin at his dad, helpless there in the next room. "What?" he said, and smiled, not really needing to know "what", or "why" for that matter, because he knew "who". It was his Dad. That was enough. His smile spread. His father drank in the radiance of that smile on the face of his son and found himself reeling. Filled with an unspeakable, dancing joy, he went to his son and took him in his arms. And they laughed. They laughed from the bottom up. They laughed from the top down. They laughed until it hurt and the tears came.

Suddenly the father said, "Let's go see your brother!"

"Great!" said his son.

"And let's take all this stuff with us!"

"Even better!" said the older son. And down the hall they went together to celebrate.

The younger, adopted son heard them from a distance, laughing as they came. "What?" he said to himself. But somehow he knew "what". He knew who was coming and somehow he knew why, though he could not have put it into words. And suddenly he became aware of a kind of rippling sensation way down deep in the pit of his stomach. He knew what was forming there and beginning to rise. And he knew that he would not resist.

Witness: Just like him. Where we're going: witness of the Father's children.

When they first arrive at Vught, the concentration camp in Holland, Betsie and Corrie ten Boom are subjected to cruel callousness, intense disappointment, endless waiting ... As time goes on there is more of the same and worse. They suffer daily humiliation, dehumanizing, brutal intimidation and extreme physical depravation. The abuse is sprinkled with bureaucratic pettiness posing as efficiency. At the end of one particularly "long day of standing, waiting, hoping", Corrie, who with all the others has been kept standing endlessly, comes to the end of her endurance as "the matron with maddening deliberateness checked off our documents against a list". She turns in utter frustration to her sister:

> *"Betsie!" I wailed, "how long will it take?"*
> *"Perhaps a long, long time. Perhaps many years. But what better way could there be to spend our lives?"*

I turned to stare at her. "Whatever are you talking about?"

"These young women. That girl back at the bunkers. Corrie, if people can be taught to hate, they can be taught to love! We must find a way, you and I, no matter how long it takes ..."

She went on, almost forgetting in her excitement to keep her voice to a whisper, while I slowly took in the fact that she was talking about our guards. I glanced at the matron seated at the desk ahead of us. I saw a grey uniform and a visored hat; Betsie saw a wounded human being.

And I wondered, not for the first time, what sort of a person she was, this sister of mine ... what kind of road she followed while I trudged beside her on the all-too-solid earth.

This older sister, Betsie, walked as Jesus walked. It was a road of suffering but it was a road of truth and love. Her heart was thankful for, and purified by the merciful love she had received. As she walked with Jesus, this purity of heart gave her eyes to see as he sees [Matthew 5:8]. She walked the "solid earth" as we all do, but she saw with spiritual eyes - he was not fooled by the mere appearance of things. She saw the things of this world from the perspective of the kingdom of God. She saw truth with the eyes of love.

Betsie and Corrie knew the suffering of their fellow prisoners because they shared it: it was a suffering in mind, body and spirit. She and Corrie reached out to their suffering sisters with kindness, prayer and the word of God. They knew where the "bread" was to be found. There in squalid barracks they were about their Father's business of feeding the hungry and bringing good news to the poor, just as they had been in Harlem.

But Betsie didn't cease to look with spiritual eyes when she looked at the guards. She saw the absolute truth: their situation was desperate. Having drunk deeply of the poison of bitterness, hopelessness and hatred, these guards were prisoners of the fear they sought to instil. They were mortally sick and tortured souls, twisting in the dark, crushed by an unimaginable weight, dead to truth and love and life itself. The guards were utterly lost. But Betsie believed that even they could have hope and a future - they were lost but they could be found. Betsie saw them with the eyes of the one who came to seek and to save the lost. Because Jesus had come for their sake, she was there - no matter where "there" was - for their sake too.

It is tempting to see Betsie, as Corry did at times, as somehow belonging to "another order of beings". This holds her at arm's length. When we view her from a distance we may tell ourselves a comfortable lie: "I could never be like that." That lie keeps our Father and the Holy Spirit at arm's length too because there is nothing Betsie was or did that every one of us cannot be and do if we allow him to draw near in love and power - if we receive the life it pleases our Father to give us.

Betsie was both safe and free in the midst of violence and death in a concentration camp. She was safe and free because she knew beyond question that she was gripped by the love and power of a perfect Father who would never let her go. The same love and power can be ours if that is what we desire; the love that makes it possible for us to love as he loves; the power to *be* as he is.

Path of the Father's Child. Freedom in the One who is truth: who we are; who he is; affirming the truth in prayer.

Questions: As you read about Betsie, did you find yourself thinking something like "I could never be like that?" Do you believe you could feel and think as Betsie did if you were in her place? Would you want to? How does your answer relate to judgement in your life? Do you want to see others with "spiritual eyes?" How is this related to your desire to see and know the Truth?

Love in Truth: The only thing that can keep us from living the life Betsie lived - the life of our Saviour - is if we want some other "life" more than we want his life.

Prayer Path:

Prayer of Petition, Affirmation & Commitment

Father, I seek now to leave the courtroom more completely behind, taking hold of the one who has come to set me free.

I believe that your love and your truth will be built up in me.

Where judgement has lived, I believe that love will have a home.

The stronghold of deception in me will weaken and fall and your stronghold of Truth will strengthen and rise.

The cursing and death I have sown and which cries out in me will be silenced by the cry of the only righteous Judge - your crucified and glorified Son!

I believe that Jesus reaped the judgement I have sown so that I can reap the blessing and the obedient life he has sown for my sake.

The place in me that has welcomed condemnation will give way to a great and mighty flood of your mercy, Father.

I will no longer seek to take by force what you desire to give me by grace.

Lord Jesus, take your throne in me:

I will receive the Father's mercy at your feet.

Come Holy Spirit, cleanse my heart.

Fill me with the Father's love;

fill me with the Father's will;

fill me with all Truth;

fill me with the heart's cry of the Beloved:

"Abba, Father!"

APPENDIX
INDEX

APPENDIX A
Courtroom Roles

Though we sit as judge - an idol in our own lives - we find ourselves
playing many if not all the roles which exist in our legal systems.
They include:

Judge

Plaintiff

Defendant

Prosecuting Barrister

Defence Barrister

Witness for the prosecution or the defence

Members of the jury

**How do we see ourselves living out these roles in the relationships
of our lives?**

APPENDIX B
Signs Of Courtroom Orientation In Daily Life

1. Everything that happens is received as evidence (we gather, weigh, etc.)
2. We are here to establish, confirm or maintain guilt or innocence
3. Concern about "rights" (under the law)
4. Accusations abound
5. The "proceedings" are adversarial … "Battlefield" orientation (use of weapons, strategies, & positions of defence and offence)
6. We cannot be vulnerable: anything we say or do may be used against us
7. Self-justification
8. Guilt and Shame worn as "clothing", not as means by which we are convicted of our sin and which lead us to repentance
9. Self-righteous indignation
10. Being offended, or taking offence for another

   Questions on our minds and hearts:

   Is this fair?
   Am I getting what I deserve?
   Have I been wronged?
   Do I have a case?
   Can I make a claim?

   All the above, applied to others …
   "Is this fair to him?
   Is she getting what she deserves?
   Has he been wronged?"   etc

APPENDIX C
Descriptions and Principles

3 Descriptions of "Matthew 7 [prohibited] Judgement"

1. Any feeling, thought, or action which takes place "in the courtroom", which is the kingdom of this world as it stands under God's judgement. "Matthew 7 judgement" is, therefore, a legal orientation and activity presided over by one who assumes the idolatrous position of "righteous Judge" over his or her own life and, therefore, over the lives of others.

2. Any feeling, thought, or action *not* done "In Christ": from a place fully informed by, and yielded to, the mercy, grace, and love of God as displayed and made available to us in the cross of Christ Jesus, who died for us when we were unrepentant subjects of sin and death. *[Romans. 5:8]*

3. 1. Human judgement of the worth or identity of one's self, another person or God.
    2. Human judgement of the motives of the heart and/or the eternal disposition of the soul.

A Few Principles

1. While I do make choices that keep me in the courtroom, it is also true that I am there by no choice of my own: I was born into the courtroom of the kingdom of this world, and that is the only place there is until Jesus makes it possible for me to come out and live "in him" in the kingdom of God. There God is my Father; he and he alone tells me who I am: his child.

2. A life free from judgement begins when Jesus *alone* is on the judgement seat of my life. That life grows, in part, from the Holy Spirit empowered choice I make to live in grateful and glad submission to God, in unpayable debt to his mercy, love and grace. In this free life, my identity, provision and purpose come from God; as he intended in my original creation.

3. Neither conscious awareness nor conscious choice is necessary for judgement to be either present in my mind and heart, or operating in my life.

4. A thought or feeling of judgement *may* arise within me, but in and of itself that thought or feeling constitutes the *temptation* to judge, not judgement (*sin*) itself.

5. *Accurate perception* of judgement present in another does not necessarily mean there is judgement in the perceiver.

APPENDIX D

Specific Judgements

Reminders: Many of the judgements we live with are received/made in childhood. We continually gather "evidence" concerning judgements which function like "answers" concerning our personal identity, provision and purpose.

Examples of specific judgements concerning the three areas of "loss":

Personal Identity

I am   a nobody   a success
           deficient   a failure
           a mistake   not loved
           better than others   not lovable
           to blame   unclean (dirty)
           bad

Provision

I am   unprotected
           in danger
           on my own

Purpose

I must do it perfectly
            be right
            get what I want
            be recognized
            be appreciated
            be successful

APPENDIX E
Key Scriptures Concerning Permitted and Necessary Judgement

Luke

12:[56]Hypocrites! You know how to interpret the appearance of the earth and the sky. How is it that you don't know how to interpret this present time? [57]Why don't you judge for yourselves what is right?

1 Corinthians

5:[12]What business is it of mine to judge those outside the church? Are you not to judge those inside? [13]God will judge those outside. "Expel the wicked man from among you."

Matthew

18: [15]If your brother sins against you, go and show him his fault, just between the two of you. If he listens to you, you have won your brother over. [16]But if he will not listen, take one or two others along, so that 'every matter may be established by the testimony of two or three witnesses.' [17]If he refuses to listen to them, tell it to the church; and if he refuses to listen even to the church, treat him as you would a pagan or a tax collector. [18]I tell you the truth, whatever you bind on earth will be bound in heaven, and whatever you loose on earth will be loosed in heaven.

Galatians

6:1 Brothers, if someone is caught in a sin, you who are spiritual should restore him gently ...

APPENDIX F

Key Scriptures Concerning Prohibited Judgement

(1) Matthew 7:[1] "Do not judge, or you too will be judged. [2]For in the same way you judge others, you will be judged, and with the measure you use, it will be measured to you. [3]Why do you look at the speck of sawdust in your brother's eye and pay no attention to the plank in your own eye? [4]How can you say to your brother, 'Let me take the speck out of your eye,' when all the time there is a plank in your own eye? [5]You hypocrite, first take the plank out of your own eye, and then you will see clearly to remove the speck from your brother's eye."

(2) Romans 2:[1] You, therefore, have no excuse, you who pass judgement on someone else, for at whatever point you judge the other, you are condemning yourself, because you who pass judgement do the same things. [2]Now we know that God's judgement against those who do such things is based on truth. [3]So when you, a mere man, pass judgement on them and yet do the same things, do you think you will escape God's judgement? [4]Or do you show contempt for the riches of his kindness, tolerance and patience, not realizing that God's kindness leads you toward repentance.

(3) Romans 14:[4]Who are you to judge someone else's servant? To his own master he stands or falls ... [10]You, then, why do you judge your brother? Or why do you look down on your brother? For we will all stand before God's judgement seat. [11]It is written: "'As surely as I live,' says the Lord, 'every knee will bow before me; every tongue will confess to God.'" [12]So then, each of us will give an account of himself to God. [13]Therefore let us stop passing judgement on one another.

221

(4) James 2:^{12}Speak and act as those who are going to be judged by the law that gives freedom, ^{13}because judgement without mercy will be shown to anyone who has not been merciful. Mercy triumphs over judgement!

(5) James 4:^{11}Brothers, do not slander one another. Anyone who speaks against his brother or judges him speaks against the law and judges it. When you judge the law, you are not keeping it, but sitting in judgement on it. ^{12}There is only one Lawgiver and Judge, the one who is able to save and destroy. But you - who are you to judge your neighbour?

(6) Matthew 5: ^{21} "You have heard that it was said to the people long ago, 'Do not murder, and anyone who murders will be subject to judgement.' ^{22} But I tell you that anyone who is angry with his brother will be subject to judgement. Again, anyone who says to his brother, 'Raca, ' is answerable to the Sanhedrin. But anyone who says, 'You fool!' will be in danger of the fire of hell. ^{23} "Therefore, if you are offering your gift at the altar and there remember that your brother has something against you, ^{24} leave your gift there in front of the altar. First go and be reconciled to your brother; then come and offer your gift. ^{25} "Settle matters quickly with your adversary who is taking you to court. Do it while you are still with him on the way, or he may hand you over to the judge, and the judge may hand you over to the officer, and you may be thrown into prison. ^{26} I tell you the truth, you will not get out until you have paid the last penny.

APPENDIX G

Key Scripture Concerning The Only Just and Righteous Judge

Acts 17:[31]For he has set a day when he will judge the world with justice by the man he has appointed. He has given proof of this to all men by raising him from the dead."

Romans 2:[16]This will take place on the day when God will judge men's secrets through Jesus Christ, as my gospel declares.

John 5:[22]Moreover, the Father judges no one, but has entrusted all judgement to the Son, [23]that all may honour the Son just as they honour the Father. He who does not honour the Son does not honour the Father, who sent him ... [26]For as the Father has life in himself, so he has granted the Son to have life in himself. [27]And he has given him authority to judge because he is the Son of Man. [28]"Do not be amazed at this, for a time is coming when all who are in their graves will hear his voice [29]and come out - those who have done good will rise to live, and those who have done evil will rise to be condemned. [30]By myself I can do nothing; I judge only as I hear, and my judgement is just, for I seek not to please myself but him who sent me.

John 12: [47]"As for the person who hears my words but does not keep them, I do not judge him. For I did not come to judge the world, but to save it. [48]There is a judge for the one who rejects me and does not accept my words; that very word which I spoke will condemn him at the last day. [49]For I did not speak of my own accord, but the Father who sent me commanded me what to say and how to say it. [50]I know that his command leads to eternal life. So whatever I say is just what the Father has told me to say."

Acts: 10: [42]He commanded us to preach to the people and to testify that he is the one whom God appointed as judge of the living and the dead. [43]All the prophets testify about him that everyone who believes in him receives forgiveness of sins through his name."

1 Peter 2: [23]When they hurled their insults at him, he did not retaliate; when he suffered, he made no threats. Instead, he entrusted himself to him who judges justly. [24]He himself bore our sins in his body on the tree, so that we might die to sins and live for righteousness; by his wounds you have been healed.

<u>Paul got it!</u>
The Courtroom Teaching in 75 Words or Less

<u>1 Corinthians 4</u>

[3]I care very little if I am judged by you or by any human court; indeed, I do not even judge myself. [4]My conscience is clear, but that does not make me innocent. It is the Lord who judges me. [5]Therefore judge nothing before the appointed time; wait till the Lord comes. He will bring to light what is hidden in darkness and will expose the motives of men's hearts.

APPENDIX H
Material for Retreat: Personal Reflection and Prayer

Purpose: To spend quiet time *with Jesus* in reflection and prayer, using any or all of the following reflection questions. You may find it helpful to keep a journal as you reflect, pray and listen. At the start, invite Jesus to be with you. Share all that you think and feel with him. Listen to him.

A. **Discovering Patterns**: When am I most apt to be "on the judgement seat"?
    (Examples to consider)

1. When I feel wronged, hurt, angry, rejected
2. When my expectations are not met
3. When my goals or desires are threatened
4. When someone I love seems to be experiencing any of the preceding (#1-3)
5. With this (these) particular person(s): _____
6. In this (these) particular situation(s) or circumstances(s):

_____

B. **Discovering Signs**: What "Signs of Courtroom Orientation In Daily Life" do I see in my life? (Refer to appendix B)

Consider each of the following relationships:

My relationship with myself (self judgement)
Other people (judgement of and by others)
God (judgement of and by God)

225

C. 1. Do you see patterns of behaviour that would indicate you are gathering evidence concerning **Personal Identity, Provision or Purpose?**

D. **Discovering With Jesus**: What do we see?

1. In view of the things you have reflected and prayed about, share your thoughts and feelings with Jesus.

2. Listen to Jesus: what does he think and feel about these things? Be aware that he may be speaking to you in his Word: what scriptures seem to be coming to you with particular power right now?

APPENDIX I

The Prayers of the Merciful Servant

Prayers of the Merciful Servant, Part I   (self)

Jesus, I know that you are making it possible for me to love myself as you love me. I thank you for your mercy, your forgiveness, your _____, and I choose, in the power of your love, to withhold nothing of you from myself: I receive your mercy; I receive your forgiveness; I receive your _____. I want to be like you: I want to be filled with mercy. In your presence I now open my hands and I release your mercy and all your gracious gifts into my mind and heart, so that I can grow into the abundant life you intend for me. Thank you, Jesus.

Prayers of the Merciful Servant, Part II   (others)

Jesus, I release these critical/judgemental thoughts and feelings to you. I turn from them and ask you to forgive me. Set me free from judgement and cleanse my mind and heart. Fill me with your love for _____. I pray that your Father's perfect will for him/her would be done, and that all the rich blessing of your Resurrection life would be _____'s, today and always.

APPENDIX J

Litany of Thanksgiving

LEADER: There is no condemnation for those who are in Christ Jesus.

PEOPLE: **Thank you, Jesus, for coming all the way to me, just as I am. I receive you as light in my darkness.**

Thank you, Holy Spirit, for pouring out my Heavenly Father's love into my heart. I want to receive you in every way that you are coming as new life for me.

Thank you, Father, for showing me that you love me, in so many ways. I want to be free from the bondage of fear. I receive your love.

L: There is no condemnation for those who are in Christ Jesus.

P: I am thankful, Jesus, that you did not come to judge me, but to save me. I receive you into the place where my heart condemns me.

I am thankful, Jesus, that you are my righteous judge. I repent of my sin. I receive the embrace of your mercy and forgiveness.

I am thankful, Heavenly Father, because you delight in me. I want to take your hand in trust. I want to walk in hope.

L: There is no condemnation for those who are in Christ Jesus.

P: I am thankful, Jesus, because you want to be with me. I want to be with you and learn from you.

I am thankful, Jesus, that you listen to me, and you speak to me. I want to learn to hear your voice. I open my mind and heart to your Word.

Thank you, Jesus, for loving me by laying down your life for me when I was dead in my sin. I choose to love you by loving my neighbour as you have loved me.

L: There is no condemnation for those who are in Christ Jesus.

P: Thank you, Precious Lord, for these Words of life. I want to walk in the light of your living Word each day. Speak, Lord, for your servant is listening.

ALL: There is no condemnation for those who are in Christ Jesus because through Christ Jesus the law of the Spirit of life set me free from the law of sin and death. **AMEN**

APPENDIX K
Daily Devotions *for* Chapters 1-9

Introduction to Devotional Materials

The following are devotional resources for the first nine chapters of *"Out of the Courtroom ..."* (Please note that devotions for the last three chapters are included within the chapters themselves.)

The material is organized with an eleven week, small group programme in view: two reading/journaling days and four days of devotions are provided for each of the eleven weeks between group meetings. The devotions relate to the assigned reading for each week and the two together provide the primary focus for group discussion, sharing and prayer.

It is suggested that the first two days of each week be given to reading the material and keeping notes or a journal of personal insight, application, etc. Devotional resources are provided for each of the other four days which include a scripture for that day, questions for personal reflection/application and prayers.

NOTE: Those reading *Out of the Courtroom, Into the Father's House* apart from a small group will want to make use of the devotional material in a way that seems best during the reading of the book and are strongly encouraged to use them in a deeper, more complete way as a follow up.

It is hoped that the teaching, the scriptures, the questions for reflection and the prayers will be places of meeting between the reader and the Living God.

Days 1 & 2

Prayers to begin the day

Jesus, Risen Lord, I open all my doors to you. Enter every room in me. As you breathed on your disciples, breathe on me so that I can receive the Holy Spirit and have your peace today.

Jesus, Saviour of the world, I release my life to you. Please bring your love and your truth into the deepest part of me. Renew my mind with your living word. Cover me with the blood of your suffering. Cleanse me with the tears of your compassion.

Jesus, Judge of all, I surrender to you as judge of my life. Fill me with your mercy. Give me your humble heart.

Reading for this week: **Introduction & Chapter 1**

("The Courtroom: A revelation")

(to be read during the first two days)

Note: Before reading, ask the Holy Spirit to open the teaching and his word to you. Pray that the scriptures and the teaching would be a meeting place for you with the Holy Spirit, Jesus and the Father. As you read, pray in response if you are lead to confess, give thanks, intercede, etc. Look up every biblical passage quoted or cited (as you read or afterward). After reading the passage, acknowledge and affirm the truth there. Pray that the word of God would be planted, take root, be watered and bear fruit for God in your mind and heart.

Daily Journal on the teaching:
Most important insight(s):

What seemed to be written just "for me" today?

What was most challenging/convicting?

What active response can I make to the "insight" and/or the "challenge"?

What was least understood/clear to me?

Prayers to begin the day (see days 1 & 2)

Scripture for today: **Romans 12:1-2**

Note: Before reading, ask the Holy Spirit to open the word to you. Ask the Holy Spirit, Jesus and the Father to meet with you in the scriptures. After reading the passage, acknowledge and affirm the truth there. Pray in response if you are lead to confess, give thanks, intercede, etc. as or after you read. Pray that the word would be planted, take root, be watered in your mind and heart and bear fruit for God.

Questions for today:

1. Have you seen the "destructive patterns of behaviour" and witnessed the consequences of "human bitterness, defensiveness, unforgiveness, arrogance, insecurity, contempt, self-centeredness and self-hatred" described in the beginning of the Introduction? Jot down a few words to remind yourself of some particular experiences you have had in the following contexts:

    (a) Family

    (b) Church

    (c) Workplace

    (d) School

2.   Consider at least one example from the previous list in which you were impacted personally. How would you describe the destructive consequences for you? For others?

Prayer Path:

Speak to Jesus about the personal experience you describe in #2 above, sharing with him your real thoughts and feeling about the people involved. Confess to him any bitterness or unforgiveness you hold against the person or persons involved. Repent of those things and ask for his forgiveness. Pray using Psalm 51:10. Ask him to heal any wounds received in your heart, mind, body or spirit. Thank him. Praise him beginning with Psalm 51:15.

Prayers to begin the day: (see days 1 & 2)

Scripture for today: **Romans 12:3**

Note: *(See note for day three)*

Questions for today:

1. According to the introduction, what is the most essential difference between the judgement which is prohibited and that which is permitted and necessary?

2. Consider this definition of the type of judgement that is "permitted and necessary": "... a biblically based discernment of good and evil concerning human behaviour - a 'judging' made in God's will and exercised to fulfil his purposes". Briefly describe a specific instance when you believe that you have made this kind of judgement.

    In what ways does your example of judgement conform or not conform to the definition?

3. Recall a specific instance when you believe you have entered into destructive, prohibited judgement of another person. Briefly describe that instance.

4. Recall a specific instance when you believe you have entered into destructive, prohibited judgement of yourself. Briefly describe that instance.

5.   Do you believe there is a connection between judging others and judging yourself? If not, why not? If so, how would you describe that connection?

Prayer Path:

Speak to Jesus about the personal examples you describe in No .3 and No. 4 above:

(a) Share your thoughts and feeling about the person or persons you judged. Confess to him any bitterness or unforgiveness you still hold. Repent of those things and ask for his forgiveness. With open hands, release your judgements to Jesus; ask to be filled with his mercy.

(b)   In Jesus' name, renounce any names you have called yourself. Renounce those names (curses) in Jesus' Name and repent of those and of any destructive judgements you have made of yourself, asking Jesus for forgiveness and cleansing. Pray using Psalm 51:10.

Prayers to begin the day: (see days 1 & 2)

Scripture for today: **Ephesians 4:17-27**
Note: *(See note for day three)*

Questions for today:

1.   What is an "idol"?

2.   What are some examples of things that function as idols in the world?

3.   Are there things which function, at least sometimes, as idols in your life? What are they?

4.   "When we enter into destructive judgement, the symptoms mask the true and desperate condition we are in: *the only Righteous Judge is not on the judgement seat of our lives.*" Do you believe that when you judge another person in the way prohibited in Scripture, you are actually taking Jesus' place as judge in your life? Do you see that this makes you an idol in your own life? If you do believe it, what might that lead you to say to Jesus? If not, why not?

Prayer Path

Ask Jesus to come and be your only judge today. Ask for the grace to receive him. Tell him of your desire to be set free of any idolatry in your life, especially judgement.

Prayers to begin the day (see days 1 & 2)

Scripture for today: **Colossians 2:6-7**
Note: *See note for day three.*

Questions for today:

1. The teaching in this book began with what the author identifies as a "revelation" from God. In view of that, what, if any, significance do you attribute to the following statement?: *"I want to emphasize that the vision and understanding that came to me was nothing new: the revelations that the Father gives to his children are not some "new" word in the sense of "adding" something to scripture."*

2. Describe an experience you have had in a relationship that felt like it was taking place in a courtroom?

3. Consider this: *"With the vision of the courtroom came an invitation: look at what goes on in a courtroom; see who is there and what they do. I began to examine my own heart with Jesus in the light of the new understanding that came as I looked."* Are you willing to personally accept the invitation to "look"? As a first step, picture a "typical" courtroom. What do you see?

Prayer Path

Express to Jesus your desire to look at your own heart and daily life *with him* in order to see the ways and means of any legal system that may be there: its procedures, objectives and, especially, the courtroom "roles" played out there. Express your desire that there would be no more "business and usual" for you with regard to judgement in your life.

Offer this season of study, meditation and prayer to Jesus asking him to be with you in love and truth.

Prayers to begin the day
(Use Prayer from Week One)

Reading for this week:

Chapter 2 ("The courtroom: life as we know it")

Chapter 3 ("The courtroom: from misdemeanour to murder")

Note: *See notes, week one*

Daily Journal on the teaching:
Most important insight(s):

What seemed to be written "just for me"?

What was most challenging/convicting?

What active response can I make to the "insight" and/or the "challenge"?

What was least understood/clear to me?

Prayers to begin the day (see days 1 & 2)

Scripture for today: **James 3:3-6**
Note: *See notes, week one*

Questions for today: (from "Fred and Jane")

1. *"So the significant thing here is not what Fred did in forgetting an appointment. The content - the significance - lies in his response to what happened ... He responds as one who sits on the judgement seat of his own life."* In Scenes 1 & 3, what specific things do Fred and Fran say and/or do which indicate that both are functioning as their own judge or as judge of others?

    Besides "judge", what other "courtroom roles" do they play? (See Appendix A)

2. In the Prologue and in Scene 4 what statements would you identify as "guilt-tripping"?

3. Does guilt have any positive function in our relationship with God? Describe that function.

    What is the difference between the "guilt" referred to in question No.3 and the "guilt" which may have been produced by the statements you listed in question #2?

4.   What courtroom roles do you observe yourself and others playing today? (See Appendix A)
     Keep a journal of these roles (with a few details about the context) throughout the week.

Prayer Path:

Lord Jesus, I commit myself to live in your light and truth today. As I look at the courtroom in the world and in me, be with me and give me eyes to see as you see. Fill me with your mercy as you fill me with your truth. I commit myself to open my hands to receive the grace I need from you in order to be cleansed from the habit patterns of sin in my life.

Prayers to begin the day (see days 1 & 2)

Scripture for today: **Ephesians 4:29**

Note: *See notes, week one*

Questions for today: (from "Fred and Jane")

1. *"Fred has failed to follow through on his promise! That's a fact."* However, every person in this little drama makes responses that illustrate ordinary, everyday destructive judgement. What would a response look like that is *not* grounded in destructive judgement and the legal orientation that comes from it? (For example: An alternative path for Fred is outlined in "Life as we know it".) How would you describe an alternative path - the way of love and truth - for:

    a. Jane in the prologue   b. Jane in Scene 2
    c. Fran in Scene 3   d. Dave in Scene 4

2. What courtroom roles do you find others and yourself playing today? Continue your journal of these roles. (See Appendix A)

Prayer Path:

Pray using 1 Corinthians 13:4-7. Express your desire to walk with Jesus in the "more excellent way". As you pray through the passage ask Jesus for the grace to love in the way Paul describes, one characteristic at a time. In each instance picture the way that is *not* love as a path. As you expresses your desire to walk the way of love instead, picture yourself turning from one path to the other.

Prayers to begin the day (see days 1 & 2)

Scripture for today: **Matthew 5:38-48**

Note: *See notes, week one*

Questions for today: (from "Fred and Jane")

1.   Do you believe there is a difference between "reacting" and "responding"? Describe.

2.   Reflect on "reacting" and "responding" in the light of today's scripture. Is there more "room" for Jesus to be *with* you in one than the other? Explain.

3.   What courtroom roles do you find others and yourself playing today? Continue your journal of these roles. (See Appendix A)

Prayer Path:

Lord Jesus, I acknowledge before you that the most important things in my life are not the circumstances or the things that happen, but who I am in every circumstance and how I respond to what happens. I do not want circumstances to dictate who I am and what I say and do. Set me free to be the person you want me to be in all that happens today.

Prayers to begin the day (see days 1 & 2)

Scripture for today: **1Peter 3:8-10**
Note: *See notes, week one*

Questions for today: (from "The courtroom: from misdemeanour to murder")

1. *"Paul reveals a fundamental aspect of that love: it does not harbour resentment or keep thinking about wrongs that may have been suffered at the hands of others. In other words, love "keeps no record of wrongs"[1Cor. 13:5]. If we are alert to this truth, we quickly become aware of times when we have begun to accumulate evidence against someone who has offended us."* Is there a person in your life against whom you believe you have accumulated evidence in the past? What were you gathering evidence about?

   Do you see any current pattern of evidence gathering against anyone? If so, what is that about?

   Has anyone seemed to be gathering evidence about you? What feelings do you have about that?

   Do you ever gather evidence about yourself? What kind?

2. Are there any relationships in your life that seem to have become, essentially, a "court case"? What would it look like for you to "drop the case"?

3. What kind(s) of "punishment" do you tend to hand out to those who have wronged, offended or judged you?

4. What courtroom roles do you find others and yourself playing today? Continue your journal of these roles. (See Appendix A)

Prayer Path:

Lord Jesus, fill me with your love today. I want to love as you love. I open my hands and my heart: I receive your patience and your kindness; I renounce and release to you my envy, my boasting and my pride. These things have felt good to my flesh, but they harm me and they harm others. I confess to you that I have held on to hurts and offences and kept a record of the sins of others. Forgive me my sin as I forgive those who sin against me.

WEEK THREE **Days 1 & 2**

Prayers to begin the day
(Use Prayer from Week One)

Reading for this week:
Chapter 4 ("The Genesis of Judgement")
(to be read during the first two days)

Daily Journal on the teaching:
Most important insight(s):

What seemed to be written just "for me"?

What was most challenging/convicting?

What active response can I make to the "insight" and/or the "challenge"?

What was least understood/clear to me?

Prayers to begin the day (see days 1 & 2)

Scripture for today: **Romans 5: 12-14**
Note: *See notes, week one*

Questions for today:

1. Have you considered that God's "No" (the things he prohibits) is just as much a part of the way he provides for and loves us as his "Yes" (the things he permits)? When and to what extent does this hold true for you when you say "no" to yourself and/or others in your life?

2. *"There in the garden we were deceived. There we disobeyed. Both are true: the deception and the disobedience."* What might the "real-life" consequences be for someone who believed that the fall of humanity was *only* due to deception or *only* due to rebellion and applied that way of looking at things to his or her own personal life?

Prayer Path:

Thank God in a simple, personal way, for what he permits and what he prohibits in your life. Tell him that you understand that both are expressions of his love. Ask the Holy Spirit to make a direct connection in your mind and heart between the Father's word "You shall not ..." and his word "I love you". Ask for the grace to love only what he loves and to hate only what he hates.

Prayers to begin the day (see days 1 & 2)

Scripture for today: **Romans 5:15-19**

Note: *See notes, week one.*

Questions for today:

1. "[The serpent tried] *to destroy [their] relationship [with the Father] by attacking its foundation, which is child-like trust and responsive love expressed as obedience."* Where would you find support for this statement concerning "foundation[s]" in the Gospels? [Hint: in a concordance, do a "word study" on: "child ("children", etc.), "love" (loves", etc.), "trust", ("trusts", etc.) and "obey" ("obedience" etc.)]? Select and write out the scriptures that seem to lend the strongest support.

2. "What might have been the reason for the use of the term "*responsive* love" in the quote above?

3. *"But the deceiver succeeded in diverting their eyes from the choice itself to some imagined future benefit."* Does this describe a way that sin operates in the world today? In your life today? Explain.

    Does the "deceiver" need to be directly involved, do you think? Why or why not?

Prayer Path:

Father, I am thankful that I can always know what is "good" and what is "evil" because you have told me in your word what things are good and what things are evil. Thank you that your words of permission and of prohibition are part of the provision that you give me as a gift so that I can live your life as your child. Thank you that you want what is best for me; that you want life and blessing for me. Give me the grace, Father, to love what is good and to hate what is evil in just the same way and for exactly the same reasons that you do.

Prayers to begin the day (see days 1 & 2)

Scripture for today: **John 1:10-17**

Note: *See notes, week one.*

Questions for today:

1. Does "good" mean exactly the same thing as "right", and "evil" exactly the same as wrong"?

    (a) If something is "good" must it also and always be "right"? Why?

    (b) If something is "right" must it also and always be good? Why?

    (c) If something is "evil" must it also and always be "wrong"? Why?

    (d) If something is "wrong" must it also and always be "evil"? Why?

2. *"The serpent's most devastating deception came in what he did not say: he failed to mention that before they could eat they would have to judge."* Does this describe the actual process we go through: do we enter into judgement of God's word before we sin in the same way that Adam and Eve did? Give a real-life example.

Prayer Path:

Lord, I want to know the truth about what is in my heart, especially concerning judgement, and I want to know it from you. I do not want to know any truth apart from you - part from your love and grace. I acknowledge and receive this truth today, Jesus: from the fullness of your grace I have received one blessing after another.

As I grow in grace and truth, let me see your glory, Lord.

Prayers to begin the day (see days 1 & 2)

Scripture for today: **2 Corinthians 10:4-5**
Note: *See notes, week one.*

Questions for today:

1. *"[Adam and Eve] start conspiring to place the blame, because that is what judges do."* When you were a child, how important do you think it was in your family to find someone to blame when something went wrong?

    Not at all _____ extremely
    (place an "X" on the line)

    How important is it for you now?

    Not at all _____ extremely

2. In terms of the means used and the ends achieved, how does "blaming" differ from a loving concern to "get at the truth"?

3. (Complete this sentence if possible) "Jesus, this is the truth: of all the people in my life, the one(s) I blame the most is/are _____, because he/she/they ..."

4. When you enter into *destructive* judgement do you think that you judge others more often as "guilty" or as "innocent"? How about when you judge yourself?

What connection might exist, if any, between your blaming someone else and your judging yourself to be innocent?

Prayer Path:

Ask Jesus to be with you as you consider your answer to #3 above. If you have not already done so, speak your answer directly to him, whether or not you are aware of his personal presence in the moment. Ask him to show you the effects of this blaming on your life. Invite Jesus to open another way for you to go, besides blaming, that would take you deeper into his truth and his love - that would bring you to a place of freedom and peace. Listen. Tell Jesus that you want to love him by doing whatever you believe he is commanding you to do. Love him. Thank him.

Prayers to begin the day
(Use Prayer from Week One)

Reading for this week:
Chapter 5 ("Do not judge": Echoes from the garden)
(to be read in first two days)

Daily Journal on the teaching:
Most important insight(s):

What seemed to be written just "for me"?

What was most challenging/convicting?

What active response can I make to the "insight" and/or the "challenge"?

What was least understood/clear to me?

Prayers to begin the day (see days 1 & 2)

Scripture for today:
Matthew 5:8; 15:14b; John 9:39-41
Note: *See notes, week one.*

Questions for today:

1. Consider the examples of the little girl who screams at her mother for being put in a "time out", and the woman who reacts to her friend's concern about her weight: in each case: a. what is her "plank"; b. to what is she blind; c. by what means does the "plank" cause the "blindness"?

2. What other kinds of "planks" are there that cause us to be "lousy" judges?

Which of these operate most often in your life?

Prayer Path:

Pray using Psalm 51, especially these verses:

1 Have mercy on me, O God, according to your unfailing love; according to your great compassion blot out my transgressions. 2 Wash away all my iniquity and cleanse me from my sin ... 10 Create in me a pure heart, O God, and renew a steadfast spirit within me. 11 Do not cast me from your presence or take your Holy Spirit from me ... 17 The sacrifices of God are a broken spirit; a broken and contrite heart, O God, you will not despise.

Close your prayer time by asking Jesus to open your eyes in any area of blindness. Thank him that he has come into the world to restore your sight.

WEEK FOUR **Day 4**

Prayers to begin the day (see days 1 & 2)

Scripture for today: **James 3:13-4:3**
Note: *See note for day three.*

Questions for today:

1. *"Destructive judgement characteristically involves a judgement of the motives of the heart and we do our judging without adequate knowledge concerning the conditions of anyone's heart."* Have you had the experience of having your motives judged? What did you feel? How did you respond? Was the motive attributed to you "accurate" to any degree?

2. Think of an instance when you judged someone ("Matthew 7 judgement") because of what you took to be their motives. Do you still believe that you were "accurate" about their motivation? Does it matter? Why or why not?

3. Using a concordance, do a word study on "slander" ("slanderous", etc.). Based upon your study, what view does scripture take of slander?

    Is it possible to slander someone with the "truth"? Why or why not?

    Is it possible to gossip about someone without slandering them? Why or why not?

Prayer Path:

Spend some time with Jesus considering with him your responses to questions #1 and #2. Ask him to reveal to you any "unfinished business" in either experience. Offer him any wounds or sin. Confess and repent of anything that needs to be confessed and repented of. Ask for and receive his healing and/or forgiveness. Close by asking Jesus to fill your heart with the motives and desires of his heart. Thank him for having the Father's heart for you.

Prayers to begin the day (see days 1 & 2)

Scripture for today: **Romans 3:22-24**
Note: *See notes, week one.*

Questions for today:

1. Have you heard others justify destructive judgement because they believe that they are not blind or ignorant - that they *do* see and know all they need to know? Have you? Describe one such example - personal or not.

2. Reflect on this statement: "I can judge myself because I know myself and am plenty aware of all the "planks" and "logs" in my eye!"

3. Have you found yourself judging another person in your heart while thinking "I would never do what they did?" Describe one instance.

4. Reflect on Jesus words: *"How can you say to your brother, 'Let me take the speck out of your eye,' when all the time there is a plank in your own eye? You hypocrite, first take the plank out of your own eye, and then you will see clearly to remove the speck from your brother's eye."* Is Jesus saying that after we take the plank out of our eye, then we can judge others?

Prayer Path:

Jesus I want to live in the truth of your word. I confess this truth to you today: there is no difference between me and the person I judge. They have sinned. I have sinned. They fall short of your glory and I fall short of the glory of God too. If I have anything good going for me so far as a relationship with you goes, it is mine as a gift of your grace. If I say that I have faith in you, Jesus, may I live that faith by extending the merciful love you have given me to others. Forgive me for thinking that mercy must be "deserved". Forgive me for living as though love must be earned. Thank you for the gift of what I need and not what I deserve or have earned. Thank you Jesus for being who you are.

Prayers to begin the day (see days 1 & 2)

Scripture for today: **1 Peter 1:13-17**
Note: *See notes, week one.*

Questions for today:

1. Have you ever said this to yourself or heard someone else say it (in effect, if not literally) "God may forgive me, but I never will"? What do you think would be the spiritual impact of living out this kind of decision?

2. What would you say, as a Christian, to someone who said "Sometimes people don't deserve mercy and forgiveness"?

3. Based on your reading, what would you say was the primary source of the destructive power of prohibited human judgement?

Prayer Path:

(a) Read Romans 5:6-11 as a prayer "personalizing" it by using "I" and "me", etc. instead of "we" and "us".

(b) Pray about someone you find hard to forgive. Again, use Romans 5:6-11 except this time substitute this person's name for "we" and "us". If this person does not profess faith in Jesus, you will want to pray portions of the scripture as intercession (ex. vs. 9), praying that God's will for them might be fulfilled in his perfect day

Days 1 & 2

Prayers to begin the day
(Use Prayer from Week One)

Reading for this week: **Chapter 6** ("Judgement: Sowing and Reaping")
(to be read in first two days)

Daily Journal on the teaching:
Most important insight(s):

What seemed to be written just "for me"?

What was most challenging/convicting?

What active response can I make to the "insight" and/or the "challenge"?

What was least understood/clear to me?

Prayers to begin the day (see days 1 & 2)

Scripture for today: **James 3:3-12**
Note: *See notes, week one*

Questions for today:

1. *"... when I receive judgement from you, I receive it as a judge. Or, to be faithful to the deeper, more scandalous implications of Jesus' teaching, we might put it this way: when I receive judgement from you, I receive it because I am a judge!"* What do you think is meant by "receive" in this sentence? Does it mean simply that I am the object of your judgement and aware that you have judged me? More than that? Explain.

2. *"The more bitterly I accuse you of being a liar, the more sensitive I become to being called a liar."* Have you observed this dynamic in yourself or in another person: you tend to be very critical of a particular behaviour in others and become very upset if you observe yourself behaving in that way or if someone else accuses you of it? Describe a specific instance if you can.

3. Could it be that the things about which we are most defensive are rooted in judgements we have made? Make a list of the things about which you are most defensive and/or sensitive.

Prayer Path:

Jesus, I give you the things I am most sensitive and even defensive about. I offer them up to you now: _____. I ask that you reveal the roots of these things to me. I release them to you and ask that you deal with them in your truth, love and power in the coming days and weeks. Set me free to receive only those things that come from your hand. I want to be free to serve you.

Prayers to begin the day (see days 1 & 2)

Scripture for today: **Galatians 6:7-10**
Note: *See notes, week one.*

Questions for today:

1. *"Once, as a young wife and mother, I was at a gathering where I overheard people talking about someone ... I never said anything. But, although I did not realize it then, I know now that my heart agreed with and took hold of that judgement."* Reflect on the truth that destructive, enslaving judgements can be embraced and have power in your heart without your ever saying anything outwardly. How might Jesus make use of your increased awareness of this possibility?

2. In what common ordinary circumstances of your daily life do you think you are most susceptible to embracing the judgements of others?

3. If possible, describe one personal example where you know (or suspect) that you have entered into a kind of silent inner agreement with another person's judgement. (Not necessarily as an adult.)

Prayer Path:

Lord, I confess the truth that you are light and in you there is no darkness. Without you I can't see what I need to see or know what I need to know. I pray that you will bring any hidden judgements in me out into your light. I believe the truth of your word that you cannot be mocked: if I sow to please my sinful nature I will experience destruction in my life; if I sow to please the Holy Spirit, the life you have given me will grow and bear fruit in your kingdom. I want to put your kingdom and your righteousness first in my life. I want to walk as a child of the light.

Prayers to begin the day (see days 1 & 2)

Scripture for today: **1Corinthians 4:12b-13a**
Note: *See notes, week one.*

Questions for today:

1. What might you say to someone who says, "If it is true that we can "agree" with a judgement and not be aware that we are doing it, then how can we possibly stop?" What would you suggest as a first step?

    What would you suggest as a second step?

2. Using a concordance, do a word study on "hidden" (hide, etc.): What stands out for you?

    (a) Do you see a connection between hiddenness and destructive judgement on the one hand and freedom in Christ on the other? Explain.

    (b) What passage was most convicting? Why?

    (c) What was most encouraging and hopeful? Why?

    (d) What do you believe Jesus is saying to you? How do you respond?

Prayer Path:

Lord, show me the path that went out from the bitterness I embraced and welcomed yesterday - show me where that path went. Show me the bitter fruit. I see the dots, Lord, but not the picture: connect the dots for me - open my eyes to see the picture - I want to see as you see and become as you are.

Jesus I confess the truth that the things I hide knowingly and unknowingly are not hidden from you. I ask that your word would be fulfilled in me so that anything concealed in me will be disclosed and anything that is hidden in me will be made known, in your perfect time.

I pray that when you come again and your glory is revealed that the resurrection life you have given to me and which is now hidden with you in the Father will rise and shine with the light of your glory.

Prayers to begin the day (see days 1 & 2)

Scripture for today: **Romans 12:9-19**
Note: *See notes, week one.*

Questions for today:

1. What do you understand a "stronghold" to be?

2. Concerning "strongholds": *(answer in your own words)* by what process does a stronghold of judgement become established in the human heart?

3. Would a faithful Christian want to rid themselves of *all* "strongholds"? Why or why not?

4. At a local town fair you overhear someone in the crowd say, "He ought to get what he deserves - what's coming to him. I want to see justice done. I want him to reap what he's sown just like it says in scripture." You (yes, you!) decide to preach on that statement the following Sunday. You deliver a "three point" sermon (it's fabulous, by the way): what are your three major points?

Prayer Path: [Romans 5:18f; 3:21-26; Philippians 2:6-8]

Father, I'm so thankful that, because you are just, you honour the sacrifice of your only begotten Son by giving him the power to reap what I have sown. Thank you that you accepted the obedient life he offered to you in love, both to please you and for my sake. Father, I am so thankful that, because you are also the "justifier", I can reap the harvest of obedient life that Jesus has sown.

Forgive me for proclaiming your justifying work of mercy in me while continuing to harbour a desire that others get what they deserve. Forgive me for proclaiming the merciful, justifying work of your Son in the lives of others while continuing to try to get what I deserve.

WEEK SIX **Days 1 & 2**

Prayers to begin the day
(Use Prayer from Week One)

Reading for this week: **Chapter 7** ("Out of the Garden")
(to be read in first two days)

Daily Journal on the teaching:
Most important insight(s):

What seemed to be written just "for me"?

What was most challenging/convicting?

What active response can I make to the "insight" and/or the "challenge"?

What was least understood/clear to me?

Prayers to begin the day (see days 1 & 2)

Scripture for today: **Romans 8:14-17**

Note: *See notes, week one.*

Questions for today:

1.   *"We were made for God. Because God is life and the source of our life, we were made in the shape of life with him. In other words, we were made in just the right 'shape' for a personal relationship with God."* Beginning with the paragraph that starts *"This is born out in our experience ..."*, find and list every specific thing (find at least 10) for which we were "shaped".

I was made for:

1._____ 2._____ 3._____

4._____ 5._____ 6._____

7._____ 8._____

9._____ 10._____

2.	Concerning the previous list: which of these things are most difficult for you to welcome and accept; in other words, which make you most uncomfortable? Why?

Prayer Path:

Pray about the things you listed in question #2. Tell the Father about what makes you uncomfortable, sharing your true thoughts and feelings about those things.

Then pray: *Thank you, Father, that you formed me perfectly for a relationship with you. I especially thank you for making me in the shape of the things which I find most uncomfortable and difficult to accept, especially*

_____

But I want to be the person you created me to be. Fill me with a greater hunger and thirst for you. Take me in your hands and reshape my heart. I am your servant, Lord. May it be for me according to your word.

Prayers to begin the day (see days 1 & 2)

Scripture for today: **1 Peter 1:18-23**
Note: *See notes, week one.*

Questions for today:

1.   Concerning personal identity: If a cross section of adults was asked "Tell me who you are without mentioning your name", what kind of answers do you think people might give?

(a) If you were asked that question, what would your answer be?

2.   Can we live without an identity? Why or why not?

3.   If God is *not* the source of our identity, what other things end up serving as the source?

4.   *"The loss of our identity puts us - and everything that is essential about us - in question. Those questions concern our being. Those questions are a deep ache, an inarticulate longing, a desperate plea: 'Who am I? Am I loved? Am I lovable? To whom do I belong?'"*

(a) What other questions do you think might be in us as a result of the loss of our created identity?

(b) Which of all the questions above concerning your identity do you think is most settled (answered) in your life in a way that you believe would please your Heavenly Father?

(c) In what way is it settled (what is the answer)?

(d) Why would this please him?

(e) Which question concerning your identity do you think is least settled in your life?

(f) Is that because it is still a question or because you live with an answer but you don't believe it is an answer that would please the Father?

Prayer Path:

Write a 1 or 2 sentence prayer of thanksgiving concerning your answer to "b" above.

Write a 1 or 2 sentence prayer of petition concerning your answer to "c" above.

Prayers to begin the day (see days 1 & 2)

Scripture for today: **1 Timothy 6:17-19**
Note: *See notes, week one.*

Questions for today:

1. Concerning provision: *"In providing for us, God our Father does not despise our physical needs, nor does he violate our created reason and will* [Genesis 3:21; Joshua 24:15; Isaiah 1:18; 6:8; John 7:16-17]." Do the scriptural references support the statement? If so, how? If not, how?

2. *"Therefore I tell you, do not worry about your life, what you will eat or drink; or about your body, what you will wear ... For the pagans run after all these things ..."* If we take Jesus at his word doesn't this mean that trust in God's provision is incompatible with such things as investments, savings and insurance? Why or why not?

3. According to the teaching in this chapter, what is (are) the deepest root(s) of our anxiety about provision? Quote the passage(s).

Prayer Path:

There are prayers that are difficult to pray with a whole heart for one reason or another. Try praying the following portion of a prayer from the *Methodist Covenant Service*. If you find yourself at odds with any of the specific commitments in this prayer, or if you find that you wouldn't actually want to receive some of the things the prayer requests of God, spend time with Jesus telling him of those things. What is he saying to you?

Father, I am no longer my own, but yours. Put me to what you will, rank me with whom you will; put me to doing, put me to suffering; let me be employed for you or laid aside for you, exalted for you or brought low for you; let me be full, let me be empty; let me have all things, let me have nothing; I freely and wholeheartedly yield all things to your pleasure and disposal.

Prayers to begin the day (see days 1 & 2)

Scripture for today: **1 Peter 3:13-17**

Note: *See notes, week one.*

Questions for today:

1. *"It was in the doing of [God's] will as they lived out their true identity as his children that Adam and Eve were to know purpose in their lives. The work that God assigned to them was not some kind of servile drudgery. It was good, creative, challenging work - a "doing" that would be both fulfilling and, especially, fruitful!"*

    Referring to the previous statement, complete this sentence: "The more I live as a child of my Father, the more I lead a life that is ...

2. What things do you do in your life that seem the most meaningful/fulfilling to you?

    (a) What things give you the greatest sense of purpose?

3. As a Christian, what do you believe is the true meaning and purpose of your life?

    (a) How does this compare with your answer to question No.2?

4. *"Instead of being an outward expression ... of our identity (our being), our "doing" becomes a means for defining, establishing and maintaining that identity."* What connection, if any, do you believe there is between the previous statement and this common experience: "I feel terrible about myself when I have nothing to do because I feel so useless."?

Prayer Path:

Lord, make me an instrument of your peace. Where there is hatred, let me sow love. Where there is injury, pardon. Where there is doubt, faith. Where there is despair, hope. Where there is darkness, light. Where there is sadness, joy. O Divine Master, grant that I may not so much seek to be consoled, as to console; to be understood, as to understand; to be loved, as to love. For it is in giving that we receive. It is in pardoning that we are pardoned, and it is in dying that we are born to Eternal Life. Amen. [Prayer attributed to St. Francis]

Prayers to begin the day
(Use Prayer from Week One)

Reading for this week: **Chapter 8** ("Into the Courtroom: The Function of Judgement in the Place of Loss") (to be read in first two days)

Daily Journal on the teaching:
Most important insight(s):

What seemed to be written just "for me"?

What was most challenging/convicting?

What active response can I make to the "insight" and/or the "challenge"?

What was least understood/clear to me?

Prayers to begin the day (see days 1 & 2)

Scripture for today: **Philippians 4:4-7**
Note: *See notes, week one.*

Questions for today:

1. How important is your need to be "in control"? (Indicate by marking with an "X")

(whatever) 1_____5_____10 (control freak)

2. In what situation(s) do you tend to try hardest to be in control?

3. During what period(s) or at what time(s) in your life did you experience the greatest loss of control?

4. Choose one from #3 above that is particularly significant: In retrospect what would you say about that period/experience in terms of:
    (a) what you did, if anything, to try to maintain/establish control?

    (b) what helped you get through it?

    (c) the lasting positive and/or negatives effects for you, if any?

Prayer Path:

Begin by praying the following prayer, then complete your prayer by listening. Invite Jesus to be with you in these questions today and in the days to come. Ask him to give you ears to hear his word to you. Do whatever he tells you to do. Seek wise counsel if you are not sure how to respond faithfully.

Jesus, I want to be with you in truth. Is it true (in some measure) that you are simply a part of my old life - that I'm still living "my old life" and not fully living your new life? Am I still in the business of trying to secure for myself what you want to give me by grace? Are you a "resource" I try to use to get the things I want or think I need? Show me the "life" I live that is not your life. Reveal the truth to me about anything I love more than I love you. Jesus, I know the truth: you are the source of any real life that I have.

Prayers to begin the day (see days 1 & 2)

Scripture for today: **Hebrews 3:12-15**
Note: *See notes, week one.*

Questions for today:

1. *"Sometimes we want what we think others have - approval, the latest "stuff", "security" - and we covet. Or it may be the other way around: we may look at one another with disdain from what we believe is a superior position. We might call this counterfeit life, 'life-by-comparison.'"*

    How much does the statement "I'm always comparing myself to others" hold true for you:

    (very little) 1_____5_____10 (a lot)
    (indicate by marking with an "X")

2. Referring again to the quote in question #1.

    (a) If and when you do compare yourself to others both in terms of what they have and who they are, are you more apt to "covet" or look down with "disdain?"

    (b) What do you covet the most? Why?

    (c) What do you have disdain or contempt for the most? Why?

    (d) In what ways, if any, do you believe your life is impacted by the things or personal traits you covet and the things or persons you despise?

Prayer Path:

Spend some time with Jesus examining your heart concerning the things you covet (consider both material and non-material things). Confess those things to Jesus. Ask for forgiveness. Receive the grace to turn from coveting to thanking. Meditate on 1 Timothy 6:6-8; Hebrews 13:5. Speak to Jesus of your desire to be filled with thanksgiving and content with what you have.

Enter in to the same process concerning those things which you disdain/despise in others. Meditate on Matthew 5:21f and Isaiah 53:3.

Prayers to begin the day (see days 1 & 2)

Scripture for today: **Ephesians 3:16-19**

Note: *See notes, week one.*

Questions for today:

1. *"The word about God's sovereignty has been sown in my heart. He is all powerful. He's in control ... It remains for me to figure out how I must be and what I must do so that he will use his power for my benefit."* How would you respond to the cynic who says that this is all any religion is about and in particular that it's what Christians are *really* up to?

2. *I trust. I pray. Many others pray for a long time. But my friend, who has said and believed and done the right things, is not healed. They said that God is "in control". Obviously he isn't. Or, more disturbing, he is and he wanted my friend paralyzed for some purpose. Though it never becomes a conscious thought, deep down in a hidden place within my heart I live in fear that God might want the same for me.* This statement is built on a number of assumptions about who God is and about how he works. List a few possibilities.

    How do these assumptions compare with the truth about God revealed in Jesus Christ?

Prayer Path:

With regard to the statement in question #2: there is fear in this person's heart. Ask Jesus to reveal any fear that may be in your heart, especially fear about who God is or what he may do. Then pray: *Lord, I open my heart to you. Sometimes I am afraid of you, and not with a "holy fear." My fear keeps me from trusting you. But I want to trust you like a child. I believe you are worthy of all my trust; heal my unbelief. I believe my fear is rooted in a lie. I want to know the truth about my heart and about who you really are. I want to experience your perfect love. I don't want to be afraid any more. Set me free. You're my Saviour. Come, Lord Jesus.*

Prayers to begin the day (see days 1 & 2)

Scripture for today: **Colossians 2:13-17**
Note: *See notes, week one.*

Questions for today:

1. *"As judges we are continually gathering evidence. In so far as we remain the judge of our own lives, everything that happens to us ... comes as evidence in the core of our being ... evidence about whether we are loved or unlovable; included or excluded; secure or vulnerable; useful or useless ..."* What is the essential difference between the gathering of evidence just described and a gathering of evidence we might undertake in order to make a permitted and necessary judgement?

2. *"Love ... keeps no record of wrongs ..."* [1Cor. 13:5]

    (a) Based upon the teaching in this chapter, why is it is so hard for most of us to love in this way?

    (b) Can you recall a time when you kept such a record of the wrongs of someone you love? What were you collecting evidence about?

    (c) When we do "keep a record" of the wrongs of *others*, what is the connection between that evidence gathering and the evidence we gather about *ourselves* - about whether or not we are "loved or unlovable; included or excluded; secure or vulnerable; useful or useless ...?" In other words, how does my judgement of you relate to my judgement of me, especially as that concerns the evidence I'm gathering about my personal identity, provision and purpose?

3. *"Even I may feel shocked by the extreme nature of my own response, and may find myself saying, "Why do I behave this way?", or, "Where did that come from?".* Are these your questions sometimes? In view of the teaching in this chapter, what steps might you take to discover the answers?

Prayer Path:

Lord, if I have accumulated any evidence of wrongs done to me, reveal it to me. I lift all such evidence to you - the things I know about and the things hidden from me. I renounce the seeming benefits of keeping these lists of offences. I confess that all this evidence simply condemns me and fills me with bitterness.

Jesus, I confess the truth that sinful humanity gathered evidence against you and crucified you. I place all of the evidence I have gathered against myself, others and against you, Lord, upon the cross of your merciful, self-giving love. Forgive me. Cleanse me. I want to love as you love. By your grace, Lord Jesus, I no longer want to keep a record of wrongs. By your grace I will walk the way of love that your mercy has opened to me. Thank you, Jesus.

WEEK EIGHT **Days 1 & 2**

Prayers to begin the day
(Use Prayer from Week One)

Reading for this week: **Chapter 9** ("In the Courtroom: *It's all about evidence*")
(to be read in first two days)

Daily Journal on the teaching:
Most important insight(s):

What seemed to be written just "for me"?

What was most challenging/convicting?

What active response can I make to the "insight" and/or the "challenge"?

What was least understood/clear to me?

Prayers to begin the day (see days 1 & 2)

Scripture for today: Luke **4:16-21**

Note: *See notes, week one.*

Questions for today:

1. Karen experienced the Father's love, but she took that experience as *evidence* that she was loved. What are the consequences for us when we experience the love of others as *evidence that we are loved*?

2. Do you see yourself collecting evidence concerning whether or not you are loved, respected, etc. in daily life? Begin to notice this common courtroom activity in yourself and others as you go through the day. Describe examples you may be aware of right at the start.

3. Three reasons are given ("The "love issue" never settled ...") as to why it is difficult for God's love to "sink in" so long as we live in the courtroom. Summarize each one as simply as you can, in your own words.

Prayer Path: (Speak truth to your own soul)

Listen, O my soul, to the truth. God is love. The God who is your judge loves you. He loves you as you sit on his throne as judge, collecting evidence about yourself and others. But he can't give you all the love he has for you if you continue to sit there in his place.

Listen, O my soul, to the truth. The one true and living God is your Father. He calls you by a name precious to him. He is patient and kind. If you turn to him and allow him to love you, you will know his patience and his warmth and his kindness toward you. If he invites you to get down off the seat of judgement, it is for your sake, not his own. He is not angry with you and he is not counting your sins. He wants life and freedom and joy for you.

Listen, O my soul, to the truth. He has preserved you for the day of salvation, freedom and life. This is the day. He has made this day for you. His hand is on you gently but powerfully. Even when you do not trust him, your Heavenly Father continues to trust that you will turn to him and receive him; he hopes when you despair; he perseveres when you give up. He will never leave you. Nothing can separate you from his love.

Listen, O my soul. Listen to your Father's heart.

Prayers to begin the day (see days 1 & 2)

Scripture for today: **Luke 4:40-44**

Note: *See notes, week one.*

Questions for today:

1. *"Right there in our hearts, alongside questions about our identity (and today's evidence concerning it) are "answers" that have come to us during our life-time - very strong evidence, if you will, that we grip, and that grips us - most especially "answers" that come to us in childhood and remain with us."*

   What "answer(s)", if any, do you believe you received as a child to the following questions:

   (a) Who are you?

   (b) Are you loved/lovable?

   (c) Do you belong/are you received and accepted?

2. Referring to question #1 above:

   (a) Which, if any, do you believe are lies?

   (b) Which, if any, of the "answers" would God the Father say "yes" to (which are true about your God-given identity "In Christ")?

3. How do you see yourself collecting evidence about these things?

Prayer Path:

(a) Lift to Jesus those things referred to in question 2a which you believe are lies about who you are (etc.) received in childhood. Renounce the lies in Jesus' name. Ask for his cleansing. Ask that where you have received lies you would now be filled with the truth from his word and as he reveals it to you personally, now and in the days ahead.

(b) Lift to Jesus those things noted in Question 2b which you believe are the truth. Affirm and give thanks for those truths. Lift up the people who have been a part of the way in which love has come to you and through whom you have come to know some of the truth of who you really are (as God created you to be).

Prayers to begin the day (see days 1 & 2)

Scripture for today: **Luke 5:17-26**

Note: *See notes, week one.*

Questions for today:

1. *"We are shaped not just by the things that happen to us, but by a number of other factors and most crucially by our response to the things that happen to us ... Sometimes a child responds to the behaviour of a parent by judging him or her ...*

   (a) How would you describe the potential consequences in later life for a child who makes a bitter judgement against a parent?"

   (b) Are you aware of having made such a judgement yourself? If so, what was the judgement and what do you think led to it?

   (c) How has that judgement impacted your adult life?

2. *Henry knew the reason why his father had left home. It was because of him; it was because Henry had left his tricycle in the driveway.* Describe any example(s) of "magical thinking" (a symptom of destructive judgement) that you see in your own life.

(a) What was the impact on you and others of this type of thinking?

Prayer Path:

"In the same way, if, as a child, I enter into bitter judgement of a parent, I live with the devastating effect of that judgement. Until and unless I renounce the curse my heart has spoken, I live under that curse." Offer to Jesus the judgement(s) you are aware of as noted in the questions above. If you are not aware of any such judgement, ask Jesus to reveal to you any judgement you may have made as a child against a parent or someone in adult authority over you. Also ask him to reveal any "magical thinking" that has functioned as destructive judgement in your life.

Pray to Jesus about these judgements: confess them; renounce them in Jesus' name; ask for forgiveness; pray for cleansing from the destructive effects of the judgement(s) for yourself and others who might have been impacted. Pray the "Prayer of the Merciful Servant [Appendix I] for those you have judged including yourself. Ask that Jesus fill you with grace and truth. Receive and affirm that grace and that truth. Receive his love. Give thanks.

Prayers to begin the day (see days 1 & 2)

Scripture for today: **Luke 4: 1-13**

Note: *See notes, week one.*

Questions for today:

Every day we are tempted to judge - to be "like God" for ourselves. In other words we are tempted to be idols at the centre of our own lives. We know that at the heart of this fallen enterprise is our desperate attempt to provide for ourselves the things we lost through deception and rebellion.

We have a companion in this life of temptation: Jesus knew the temptation we know. In fact, we know that he was tempted in every way just as we are [Hebrews 4:15]. So we know that Jesus too was tempted to enter into destructive judgement - to set himself up in the business of trying to secure for himself what the Father wanted to give him by grace: personal identity, provision and purpose. Today's scripture is a record of a time of profound temptation at the start of his earthly ministry.

Reflect on the temptation of Jesus as recorded in the forth chapter of Luke. Is this a record of Jesus being tempted with regard to personal identity, provision and purpose?

What connections do you see? Explain.

Prayer Path: Meditate on and pray into the words of scripture Jesus speaks in response to the devil's temptations.

1. "Man does not live on bread alone." [Deuteronomy 8:3]

2. Worship the Lord your God and serve him only" [Deuteronomy 6:13]

3. "Do not put the Lord your God to the test." [Deuteronomy 6:16]

WEEKS NINE THROUGH ELEVEN

Devotional material for the last three chapters is included within each of the chapters themselves. The reader in encouraged to use the material in the immediate context as the chapter is read.